Expulsion

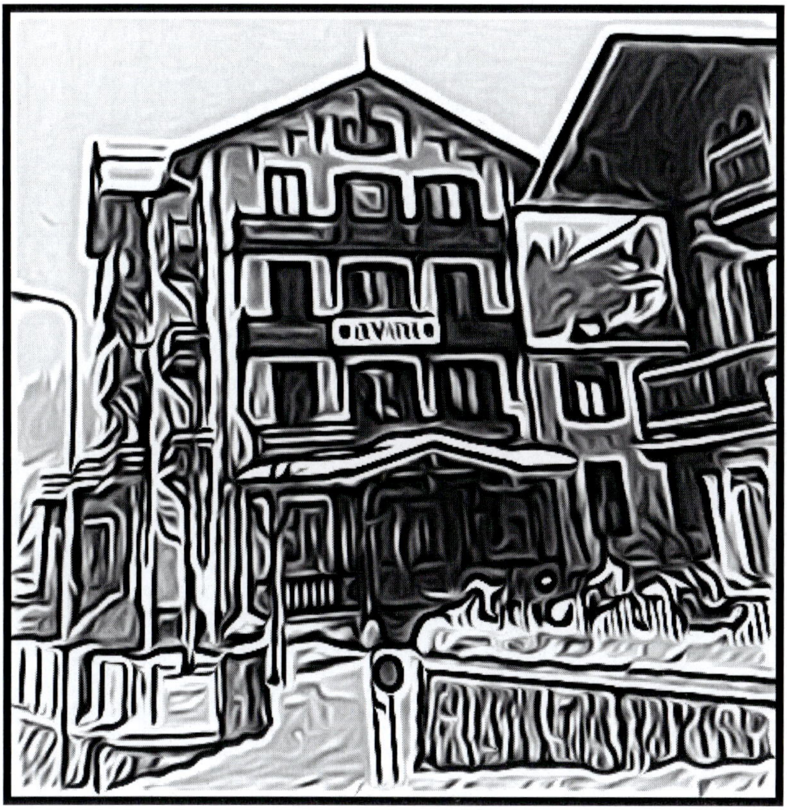

A Memoir by

Madeleine King

Calgary, Canada

2020

Happy reading!
Madeleine
Aug 2020

King, Madeleine, 1946 -

      Expulsion – A Memoir by Madeleine King

ISBN: 978-1-71679-309-7

First printing in July 2020 by Lulu.com

Cover Image: © Madeleine King – Created by R.W. (Bob) Taylor, the author's husband, based on a photograph taken by the author while attending the Institut La Villan School in Switzerland.

Dedication

This memoir is dedicated to my late parents, Sonya Coleman and Lewis Cohen, Lord Cohen of Brighton, and to my wonderfully supportive husband Bob Taylor. His love helped me find the courage to search for meaning in experiences.

Without the patience, wisdom and insight of Donna Friesen and Nick Coleman I could not have and written so much.

" Love to pray. For prayer gives a clean heart. And a clean heart can see God."
Mother Teresa

Madeleine King

Contents

Chapter 1 – Where it All Began

When I was 14 years old I was expelled from a boarding school in Switzerland, accused of being the worst troublemaker in the school. They said I was a bad influence on the other students.

All the assembled staff and students heard this cruel condemnation. When I was told I could nevertheless stay, I could not imagine what kind of teenager could stay in a place where they had been so publicly condemned. Having been confined to the school building, I packed my bags and escaped by climbing out of the window to travel home alone to England.

This is a story of my search for ways to prove this assessment wrong. I have done this by finding opportunities to use my gifts for good and not for ill. The journey took me from mischievous teenage years through educational challenges to family life and a variety of careers.

Along the way experiences kept changing me in ways unimagined by my teachers at that school in Switzerland.

How many of us during our teenage years find the rules and expectations of those exercising power over us unreasonable, leading us to challenge society's norm? This small memoir looks at the nature

Expulsion

of those challenges, and to what extent the predictions of our elders help us in our struggle to find our true nature.

I had been born in 1946 in our family home in the Sussex village of Ditchling, about eighty kilometres due south of London. My mother was 33 and my father 49, my brother 6 and sister 4 years old. When my parents had bought the house, called Lattenbells, soon after they were married, my father, a well-known businessman, town councillor and aspiring socialist politician moved from nearby Brighton while my mother had lived in London. Unfortunately, their marriage fell apart soon after my birth, with my parents separating, and divorcing some years later.

After my parents' separation my mother took sole responsibility for the care of us three children while my father was always financially reliable and generous. She took us to live in California while my father returned to Brighton. This was a time of considerable instability for us as she struggled to cope with single parenthood and her search for a place to call home.

Redwood Studio
Santa Cruz

After a year in America we returned to our family home of Lattenbells for one winter, during which my mother was very unhappy. The following spring, with me only two years old by then, she took us three children to South Africa, where we lived in Cape Town for the next five years. Despite the circumstances I was a happy and gregarious child.

In 1953 we returned from South Africa to Lattenbells which had been rented out during our absence, and then renovated enlarging it to a five-bedroom home.

Lattenbells, Ditchling, Sussex, UK

Our return was so that we three children could attend private boarding schools (confusingly known as public schools). At that time, it was the preferred path for parents who could afford the fees and wanted the best all-round education for their children. My brother and sister went away immediately and spent the next few years at boarding schools, whilst I lived at home with my mother for the next five years while attending local private day schools.

Our Family: Myself, John, Mother, Christine, Father

~

Chapter 2 - English Boarding School

To understand what circumstances led me to attend school in Switzerland we must go back a little.

I was twelve when I followed my sister to Roedean, one of England's foremost girls' boarding schools. The school building is situated just east of Brighton, high up on the cliff top, looking due south over the English Channel so that on a clear day you can see France. It was built as a school in the late 1800s and looks dark and bleak and imposing. The academic portion is a long rectangle lying perpendicular to the coast, with the four residential "houses" jutting forward in a methodical pattern. In each one, about eighty girls, their house mistress and their matron reside.

The foundational Victorian ethic of the school was to demonstrate that girls are as tough and capable as boys. In order to acquire the famous British "stiff upper lip" it was considered beneficial to subject students to the rules and authority of the staff and senior students with the exception of only four family day visits during a typical three-month term. This meant that although my mother was living only twelve kilometres away and my father in Brighton, yet I was unable to see them during each term except for my four day-outings. My sister was a prefect and therefore had to discipline and reward us younger students; being afraid to show any favouritism, she leaned the other way and was careful to avoid being someone I could turn to for advice and support.

There was a lovely Church of England chapel and cloisters attached to the back at the west end. Our school principal (headmistress) was so deeply religious that in one of her inspirational sermons she told us that it was only God you could truly love; never a man! Another aspect of our times in the chapel was that during services girls frequently fainted and had to be carried out due to the noxious fumes that came up through the vents.

All the girls shared bedrooms with one or two others of their choice. Our situation felt more complex because my best friend Ginny and I were terrified we might be forced to share a room with our classmate Leonora. From time to time Leonora had epileptic fits in our presence, even once while visiting our bedroom, foaming at the mouth, physically contorted, and imbued at those times with enormous strength. Unfortunately, the school authorities failed to tell us that it was epilepsy, or to give us any information as to how we should handle it when we were alone with her. Most importantly they never reassured us that no student would ever have to share a bedroom with her.

My favorite times were in the tiny bedroom I shared with Ginny. The room was just big enough for two narrow beds, bedside tables, chests of drawers and wardrobes, with virtually no floor space. Our beds were as narrow as sleeping bags, with course horsehair mattresses, lumpy pillows, plain white cotton sheets and three or four rough wool blankets. Often the rain came in, dripping down the inside of the windows and pooling on the floor, and when it was windy at night the windowpanes woke us up with their rattling. In fact, the school was so cold that ink sometimes froze in our inkwells, which is significant since ink freezes at a lower temperature than water. Ginny and I consoled ourselves with the knowledge that all this would make us strong and resilient forever! Like having to eat every single scrap of food that was put on our plates, whether we wanted that quantity of food or the particular choice for that meal. Or having to submit ourselves to the terrifying authority of Muck, the Matron of our House, a nurse by profession who took on such tasks as insisting exactly how we were to behave while taking a bath; dry ourselves while standing in the bath so that the bath mat was not wet for the next bather, or how we were to make our beds every morning by using neat "hospital corners" (before fitted sheets and duvets were available).

My friendship with Ginny made all these hardships part of a fun experience. Her family, who had a dairy farm north of London, with an older brother and sister, were all sex mad. They loved each other passionately and all of them seemed to be constantly talking and thinking about sex, which was a fabulous contrast to my own family. In our room we listened to Elvis Pressley and the first British pop music on Radio Luxembourg and pirate radio stations, which delighted us by breaking with tradition. Ginny smuggled into school a copy of Lady Chatterley's Lover by D.H. Lawrence which had just survived a notorious censorship case on the basis of the explicit sexuality being an integral part of a work of fine literature. The literature aspect probably escaped us, but we certainly did enjoy reading it, and were happy to let other girls know all about our discoveries. Outside our window there were workmen doing outside work on the building. We enjoyed ourselves innocently flirting with them through the window; so much so that the house mistress decided our fun needed to be stopped, and she sent the workmen away part way through their contract, delaying the work until we were home for the holidays.

One day in December 1959 I was sitting eating afternoon tea in the dining room with my friends when our daily post arrived. There was a letter from my mother, which was not unusual, as we wrote each other three or four times a week; but it was the contents of this letter that made it stand out for me.

My Darling Madeleine,

I'm so sorry to hear that you're having such a bad time with your nose and being completely stuffed up for so long. And now you tell me your neck is sore with swollen glands. I hate to hear that you're so miserable with it all.

I've made an appointment for you to see the allergy specialist in London next Monday.

Be sure to be ready when I pick you up at 9 o'clock so we'll be in good time to catch the train to London.

Sending you lots of love and hugs and kisses,

Mom

Naturally I was delighted that my mother had heard my pleas for help, and I travelled with her to London in a state of excitement wondering what would be in store next.

I had arrived at Roedean with a new teddy bear that had been made at my mother's arts and crafts school in Brighton. That gift changed my life, and not for the better. I became very allergic to its kapok filling, and once my nasal allergies had been triggered, they reacted to a host of different stimuli. In an era before antihistamines became available, I was prescribed a course of de-sensitizing injections to be administered by me. Twice a week I would walk to the school sanatorium where I would sterilize a multi-use needle, fill the container to the required level and inject it into my upper leg. Always I was scared, sometimes the needle was too blunt to pierce the skin and would have to be changed out for another after several attempts, and often following a successful injection my leg would swell up and be sore for a day or two. On one occasion I managed to hit a blood vessel so that I turned blue and was diagnosed as being in medical shock. It was all a misery.

Expulsion

Having arrived at London's Victoria Station after an hour's train journey, my mother and I took a taxi to Harley Street where the top English medical specialists saw private patients in beautiful historic row houses. My mother had arranged for me to see one of Britain's few allergy specialists of that era. The specialist put drops of different allergens all down both of my arms and over my whole back and then pricked each one with a sharp needle. By examining the ones that almost immediately became red and itchy she could tell whether the injections were reducing my sensitivity and what I was now allergic to. The news was not good at all; I was even more sensitized than before starting the injections, and I was now allergic to a wider variety of substances.

The specialist seemed deflated by the whole process as she pronounced that all she was able to suggest was that perhaps the English air was bad for me, and my parents should consider moving me out of the country. My mother and I were stunned. This was hugely disruptive.

We had been back in England for six years. Academically I was doing very well at Roedean, having finally adjusted to the English system after my educational start in South Africa, and was now amongst the top students in all categories including Classical Greek, Latin, Physics and Mathematics. My brother had successfully completed his English public-school education and had recently left for McGill University in Montreal, while my sister had the remainder of her final year at Roedean. I could sense that my poor mother felt completely out of her depth and would need to discuss the situation with my father. Luckily despite having divorced they remained on very friendly terms.

I returned to Roedean later that day, sworn to secrecy about the outcome of the appointment since my parents did not want any of the staff or my friends to know that it was questionable whether I would be able to return to school following the approaching Christmas holiday.

By the time I came home for Christmas my parents had made a plan. We were to leave almost immediately for a skiing holiday in St. Moritz, Switzerland, after which my father and sister would return home while my mother and I visited various Swiss schools until we found one that would take me in straightaway. It was to be a whole new experience in my life and I had no idea what to expect; I felt fear of homesickness and losing my friends, while also being exhilarated by the newness of it, the chance to ski almost every day, and delighted by the prospect of being able to breathe properly again in the clean Swiss air.

~

Chapter 3 - Incident at the Swiss School

Following the Christmas festivities at St Moritz, when I was fourteen, my mother and I visited several schools until we found a small school called Institut La Villan in a tiny village up the mountain from Villars, a ski village perched above Montreux and Lausanne. It was a typical Swiss style building with four stories, wooden shutters, and balconies. There was a spacious central section of the main floor, which was the dining and study area, where students were happily congregated. The classrooms opened off this space in all directions.

My mother and I found the atmosphere warm and welcoming, and so it was decided that I should start immediately while she returned to England.

Unfortunately, and unappreciated by us at the time, the owner and principal had died suddenly just two weeks before my arrival. The school was now being run by his widow (Madame Palisch) who had no relevant experience or ability but had been left with five children of her own to support.

Institut La Villan

There were about forty students, most of whom were the children of American academics taking European sabbaticals. I was the only student from England – and for many students I was the first English friend they had ever had. Discounting the fifteen juniors with whom I had little connection, there were thirty of us teenagers aged fourteen to sixteen, in a co-ed boarding school a long way from home. It was not surprising that we had a lot of fun! At the same time, in typical teenage fashion it was a time of heightened emotions, mood-swings and misbehaviour of all sorts.

Expulsion

I shared a room with Marion, the bright and lively daughter of a Stanford professor. She and I used to fantasize about our teachers; they came from different countries and appeared to have had questionable career paths before teaching at La Villan. We developed the notion that in secret they were an international spy ring, and we allotted specific governments to each of the key teachers. Naturally, there was for instance a Nazi spy and a Japanese spy. It was a fun game, and I wrote all of it down in a diary.

In the spring after a month of treatments at home in England for a knee injury that I had sustained in a ski accident I returned to our room. When Marion complained about my snoring, I said it was not me who snored; I claimed that since my leg was protected from the

weight of the bedlinen by a medical cage, that allowed me to hide a lover under my bedclothes, and it was he, not me, who was snoring.

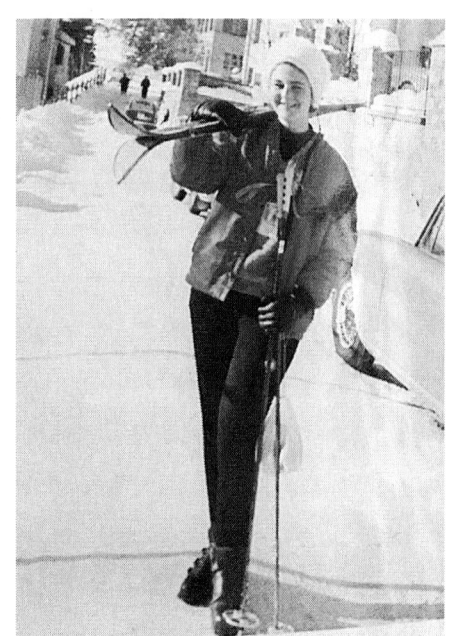

I was very social and totally boy mad. I had fun with a new practice whereby at night boys would lower a basket from their bedrooms on the top floor to our window, with messages for their girlfriends to be delivered by me or Marion before the following morning. That turned out to be a first step in night-time antics. Our bedroom was the only one on the girls' floor without access to the huge balcony running the entire length of the building, with a fire escape coming down from the boys' floor.

By late spring we heard via some very reliable sources that three or four boys had, by prior arrangement with their girlfriends, dared to climb down from their floor to the balcony outside the girls' floor and into their rooms. It turned out that this was so courageous for the boys involved that when they were in their girlfriends' rooms, they were much more timid than they were during our many school dances. They could not even rustle up the courage to kiss or hold hands.

By way of celebrating our time together I wrote my diary as a gift to Marion describing all the excitements of our shared experiences. One of its aspects was that it faithfully chronicled who was dating who and who had started climbing down the fire escape at night. They were named! Unfortunately, I neglected out of mistaken respect for the timidity of the boys, to include the fact they were too scared even to kiss the girls let alone do anything more.

One day in May my diary went missing. I had made the mistake of writing it in an exercise book identical to ones we used for our homework. Anxiety overtook us. Who had it? Who was reading it? Were one or more students enjoying the gossip it contained, or was it in the hands of a teacher? How angry might a teacher be?

Expulsion

One day passed and then two and then three. The suspense was extreme. Then we heard there would be a full staff meeting after supper during "study hall" when all students were assembled together. After about half an hour, I was called in to the adjoining room where the staff were meeting. All the students watched this unique happening of a student being summoned to enter a staff meeting.

As soon as I was in the room Madame Palisch and the teachers started questioning me about the contents of my diary. All my lame attempts at teenage humour were thrown in my face and turned against me. They blamed me for callously taking advantage of my parents following my ski accident by unnecessarily encouraging them to fly me home. Regarding my imaginary lover who snored, they accused me of really having a lover in my bed.

We students often lost possessions from our closets for which we blamed the foreign maids who cleaned our rooms. The mention in my diary of this accusation caused the teachers to accuse me of doing the stealing myself, of being a thief. Turning to our spy ring, we had chosen to pair each teacher with a country whose most unpleasant national characteristics seemed best to suit their persona. This angered my teachers the most.

The worst part of this "inquisition" came when they turned their attention to my description of the boys visiting the girls' rooms at night. Having reduced me to a tearful wreck, the teachers called in each of the boys I had mentioned followed by the girls, accusing each one of having sex. I was in the room the whole time. None of them knew before that moment that their names and activities had been included in my diary. As each one entered the room they looked inquiringly towards me, making me feel ashamed of having landed them in this situation. The boys were horrified, while the girls were mortified at having been publicly accused of having lost their virginity – none of which was the least bit true. One girl even offered, through her tears, to submit herself for a medical examination to prove her innocent status.

I was accused of being a liar, a cheat, and a thief, and being responsible for all the bad behaviour in the school exhibited by both girls and boys. Every single student named in my diary was expelled that night – about one third of all the students. The majority being American, they were utterly scared they would lose their grades and have to repeat the year on their return back home.

The night that followed was a disaster. Marion and I whispered to each other from our respective beds until the early hours. We went over and over how it could have come to this, how my parents would react, how it would affect each of the students and what the immediate future would look like. In the hours that followed I tossed and turned until dawn finally broke. I was hugely anxious about how the day would unfold.

Amazingly when we woke up the next morning all the expulsions had been cancelled, all communication with our parents forbidden and we were placed in a lock-down with no-one allowed to leave the building. Chaos reigned with no-one knowing whether we were coming or

Expulsion

going. Several of the girls were hysterical and had to be put on tranquillizers.

Me looking out the "Window of Escape" in happier times.

There was no way I could envisage staying in a place where I had been accused of such dreadful things. So, I climbed out of the window, walked into the village, and since my mother was travelling abroad. I called my father in England. My father told me that if I could get on a train down the mountain to Geneva there would be an air ticket awaiting me at the airport.

With that assurance I climbed back into the school, packed my bags, and said a fond farewell to Marion and other friends. Many of them handed me supportive letters, and most gave me their home addresses inviting me to come visit them in the States.

Next I went to say good-bye to Madame. She was surprised to see me in her office of my own volition, and even more surprised when I told her that I was about to quit the school that minute and that it was for ever. Much to my surprise she was horrified; she tried in vain to persuade me to stay. There was no way I could accept her change of heart.

Alone, at fourteen, I took the train down the mountain, changed trains at a couple of stations, and once in Geneva, found my way to the airport and the waiting ticket that my father had promised.

One student had handed me a letter before I left the school saying it was to be opened only when I was on the plane.

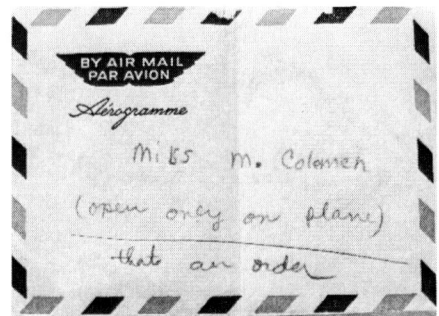

The letter (a copy of which follows) describes me as something of an idol ("idle"). At the time it was impossible for me to accept the compliment when I had been made to feel that I had created such havoc!

Expulsion

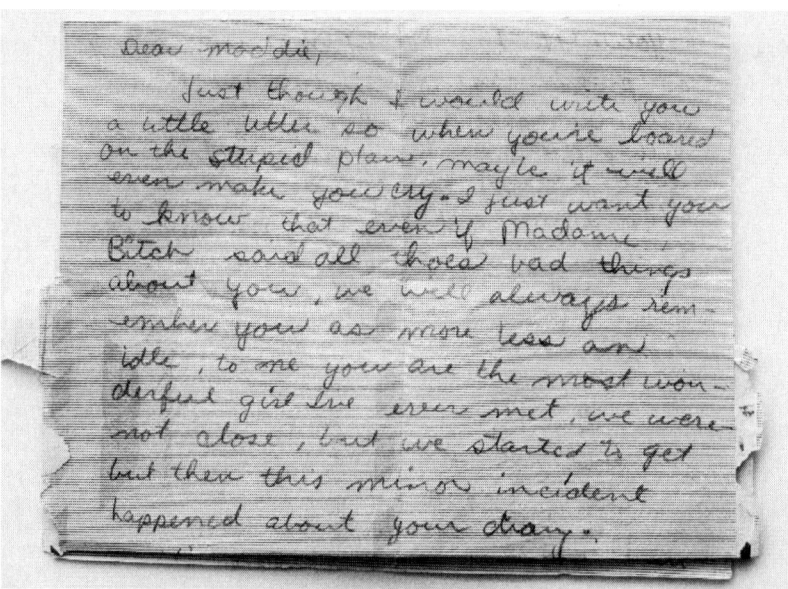

During my journey Madame phoned my father to warn him not to believe anything I said, and she repeated her awful assessment of my character – and he believed her. And so, in my shame and misery, I was met by my father who took me to his home, the only time in my life I slept at his house.

From that moment I worried that he believed I was destined to end up "in the gutter" as Madame Palisch had warned him, with my family ashamed of me and my life in ruins.

~

Chapter 3 – Return Visit to Madame

After my expulsion, it seemed that my parents were in a constant state of confusion as to what sort of a person I was. Had I really been a bad troublemaker at the Swiss school? And was that going to be my life's journey – that those I loved would be forever ashamed of my behaviour? I was horrified at the thought that I might turn out to be a disgrace to my parents. I loved and respected my mother. I knew my father less well, but I was proud of him having been a well-loved and jovial Mayor of Brighton, founding chairman and president of one of the country's largest building societies and an important voice within the Labour Party.

When my mother returned from her travels a couple of weeks later she collected me from my father's house and took me back to our family home. Unlike my father, she did not leap to the conclusion that I was at fault. She quietly gave me her full attention and coaxed me to share with her my side of the story. Having listened to my explanation, she surprised me by insisting that we go to the school to confront Madame over what had happened and to retrieve my diary. She explained that I needed to apologise for what my actions had caused, even though as it turned out I was the only student who left the school as a result of the incident.

Expulsion

We duly travelled to the school and met Madame in her office. The previous time my mother and I had entered that building together the atmosphere had seemed warm and friendly with students milling happily in the main central area, and that was what had attracted us to it initially. Now the building loomed large over me as we entered the doors, and I felt terrified of making eye contact with any of the students. Luckily, Madame's office was immediately to the right of the door, so we did not need to venture into the main space. My mother explained to Madame that she had brought me there both for me to apologise for the upheaval that had been caused and also to retrieve the diary that rightly belonged to me. She coaxed me to apologise. Madame explained that the school was her only income and if the diary were read by the authorities, she was afraid she would lose her licence. She therefore refused to hand over my diary. Much to our surprise, she lit it on fire, dramatically burning it to ashes while we stood watching so that no one would ever again know its contents.

That fall I heard that the school unexpectedly closed down forever during the summer. The news confirmed my suspicion that Madame had hated managing the school, and that she had done so only during the short time it took her to find a new husband to support her. That summer she married the local hairdresser.

Unfortunately, none of that understanding removed my teenage sense of shame.

~

Chapter 4 - Speed Boat in the South of France

On leaving the school, my mother and I holidayed in the South of France near Monte Carlo. We fell in love with it and found a beautiful villa to buy, on a cute little peninsula called Cap d 'Ail overlooking the Mediterranean, with Cap Ferrat on the horizon. Canadian media baron Roy Thompson had the magnificent villa next door and iconic film star Greta Garbo also had her villa there. We called ours "Villa Serena", and spent many summers there, although few of them turned out to be serene.

Villa Serena – Cap d'Ail

When my mother and I came back to England a few weeks later, my parents (Mom and Pop as I then called them) surprised and delighted me by giving me the gift of a speed boat. I can only imagine that their decision must have come about through a conversation something like this:

Expulsion

Pop: *I'm really worried about Madeleine. She's out of control. If she doesn't pull herself together and get serious she'll end up a total mess. Her choice in friends is awful, and she's such a wild teenager. She won't listen to me, so there's not much I can do. You need to keep her close to you, so she doesn't go off the rails.*

Mom: *She's had such a rough time. She's a good girl and I think she's smart like you. I'm sure it'll all turn out ok. And your financial help and support will make it easier for me. In fact, I'm worried that she'll get bored having two months of a beach holiday at the villa each summer. You remember how much she loved the water-skiing when we were all in Italy last year? Well I've been wondering if you'd buy her a boat so she can waterski to her heart's content. And the boat will give her something to be responsible for. What do you think?*

Pop: *Well that's not a bad suggestion, and business is going quite well at the moment so I think we could do it. In fact, the Boat Show is coming up next week – so why don't we go and maybe we'll find one there for her and then you can drive it down to the Mediterranean with you.*

My brand-new fibreglass boat with an outboard motor powerful enough for water skiing and four fancy reclining seats, was named "Araminta". I moored her at a buoy in the bay below the villa.

Everyday those of us who were staying at the villa would cross the tiny road that looped right around our house, climb down the rough staircase opposite, hugging the steep slope down the hundreds of steps to the beach. There I spent nearly all my days.

Enjoying the beach at Cap d'Ail

There was an open restaurant at the back of the beach where my mother had an account for the whole summer, so I could eat and drink whatever I wanted.

The beach was a wonderfully social place, and Araminta made me especially popular. I loved taking young people for rides and letting them water-ski, and I let my friends drive the boat for me to water-ski.

As a boat owner I was somewhat over-confident given that I was only a fifteen-year-old with no boat training or previous experience whatsoever. Knowing nothing of the rules of navigation, I drove her into Monte-Carlo harbour at about twenty miles per hour. I was met with screams of concern and abuse from all sides.

Expulsion

On one occasion I was so busy chatting with my friends on board that I took both hands off the wheel to raise them high and wide while I regaled them with a story. To much laughter from my passengers, I lost my balance and fell backwards into the Mediterranean. One of my passengers was kind enough to take the wheel and circle the boat to collect me.

On a more serious note, during a bad storm the men on the beach told me my boat needed to be brought in to the beach so it did not get bashed to pieces on the rocks. They were all enjoying their big lunchtime meal and so they could not go in the water. There was no-one swimming, and no one else on the beach who might help me. I duly swam out alone the hundred metres to where Araminta was tied to the buoy. The waves were huge, and when I arrived the boat was crashing up and down and I realized with terror that it might easily swing round and crash down on me. I screwed up my courage and athleticism managing to throw myself over the edge and land in a heap on the floor. Next, I had to climb onto the bow, reach the very tip of the prow and untie the rope attaching it to the buoy. As soon as I climbed onto the bow I clung onto the top of the windshield for dear life, realizing there was nothing else to hold onto to reach the front point. The waves were crashing up and down and every second seemed like a miracle that I could still hold on. I moved back onto the floor and sat there crying my eyes out at the hopelessness of my situation and praying fervently for deliverance. There was no-one who would rescue me. I could not untie the boat and drive it to safety on the beach. Eventually I realized that my life was more important than saving the boat. If I were to swim all the way back to the beach I would need every once of my strength. Since my crying was weakening me, I needed to pull myself together and stop both crying and praying right away. This whole time I was the only person in the water in the whole bay. I left the boat still tied to the buoy and struck out for shore. The swimming was very tough. When I reached the shore I was so fatigued that I just let the waves draw me onto the beach and then drag me back out again, with no energy to pull myself out of the water. Eventually the men, whose meals were long finished, pulled me out and revived me with brandy as I lay prone on the pebbles.

Miraculously Araminta did survive that storm, although a subsequent storm eventually put an end to all the fun I had had with her.

With my friends from England who camped nearby, and my older siblings and their friends, we made quite a social group. We made friends also with a group of local young men who loved to party. One night we went to a party in an abandoned castle. The stone staircase had fallen into ruin, but we managed to pick our way through the rubble to the open roof. There was music from someone's boombox and glorious views over the rooftops and down to the sea, and lots of wild young people. Most people brought wine but inevitably there was at least one bottle of the hard stuff which made many of us drunk. At the end I came home with a local French group doing four-wheel skids all the way down the famous switchbacks into Monte-Carlo. The next night we partied at a beautiful apartment in the heart of Monte-Carlo, where for the first time I saw two lesbians enjoying each other fully

Expulsion

clothed but lying on a bed together in the middle of the central area of the party. At that party there was also a Swedish nymphomaniac, who spent the entire evening passionately kissing and fondling one guy after another. I was amazed by what was happening around me, and deeply uncomfortable, but had to wait until the end of the party for someone to take me home. The following night the party was on the mountainside above Menton, just east of Monte-Carlo, as it sloped steeply down towards the Mediterranean with the bright reflection of the moon shining on the calm water. My problem that night was that for the first time I encountered a sex maniac (as we called them in the early sixties) who could not keep his hands off the girls, and from whom I spent the whole evening fleeing in terror.

These parties were glamorous, but I was much younger than everyone else, and I was in "way above my head". For the boys, the only question was who they would hook up with that night. Since, like most of my girlfriends back in England, I prized my virginity, it made it tough to enjoy partying with this crowd.

~

Chapter 5 – The Smugglers' Snuff

Back in England, during the years when I was fifteen, sixteen and seventeen, my social life was less constrained as I relaxed among my peers. I became a founder member of a youth club in my village of Ditchling called The Smugglers' Snuff. We made music tapes on my father's old Grundig reel-to-reel tape recorder that were great to dance to, served food and non-alcoholic drinks and enjoyed a safe social place every Friday evening in an ancient disused abattoir, all without adult supervision. It became so popular that we drew crowds from far and wide.

Ditchling was famous for its pubs and although we were not officially allowed to drink until eighteen, my friends and I were frequent customers enjoying draft beer. The village had never encountered teenagers like us, and we got thrown out of several pubs for random misdeeds like kissing or holding hands. I felt I was part of a generation that was determined to live life by our own moral code, and the older generation were stuck in their ways and having a very hard time trusting us in our exuberance.

One Maundy Thursday (the Thurssday before Easter) my mother dropped me off in Brighton as I had told her I wanted to do some

Expulsion

shopping. In fact, I went straight to the pub where my friends congregated. Arriving before them, I was standing outside when a man pointed me out to his young son as a girl who hangs around bars hoping to pick up guys, possibly a prostitute and not someone he should ever associate with. I was disgusted with his comments but did not care about his mistaken views. Unfortunately for me he, like many in Brighton, knew whose daughter I was – and so the story was reported to my father.

When my friends did arrive, we decided to go for a spin in the country in a friend's new red convertible MG Midget. The weather was glorious, so one of the boys and I sat on the back trunk with our feet on the minimal back seat while another boy had the only other girl on his lap in the passenger seat. This was of course long before seat belts had been introduced. The young driver drove so fast that when we stopped to enjoy a Sussex cream tea in a pretty village, the boys took him aside and told him he was trying too hard to impress us girls and that he was endangering us all. It was shortly afterwards that he took a corner too fast and lost control. The car tipped over and we were all thrown out. Amazingly we landed on a grass verge, so no-one was killed, although we were all quite severely injured. Despite my suffering what turned out to be a fractured pelvis, I was not bleeding like the others, so during the ambulance ride I had to sit up front, next to the driver on a hard bench seat.

When my mother received the phone call from the country hospital some 40 kms from Brighton, her biggest upset was that I had misled her, leading her to believe I was shopping on my own in Brighton. She may even have felt that I had deliberately deceived her if I had known I would be going on an outing with my friends. Even so she forgave me and was her usual supportive mother. In fact, she was so keen that I would not get lonely and bored lying flat on my back for a month in a hospital ward amongst rows of beds filled with seniors at the end of their lives, that she bought me sexy nightgowns so that more boys would want to visit me!

She and my father were definitely right to worry about me. When my mother left me at home at Lattenbells while she went out during the day I used to climb the roof of our two-storey house. It had lots of gables and other interesting angles and was steep enough to provide some real challenges. Another risky behaviour was hitch-hiking alone. Ditchling was some twelve kilometres from Brighton and there was only one bus every hour or two, and it took a full forty-five minutes to arrive, double the time to make the journey by car. When hitch-hiking I often got picked up by men on their own. Much to my surprise several of them expressed fatherly concern at the risk they considered I was taking and would make me promise not to hitch-hike alone in future. I found their concerns heart-warming, but they did not influence my behaviour in the least.

Sometimes I would cycle to the next small town of Hassocks and get the train from there, but shortly after I started doing that, I left my bike at the station unlocked for a few days. I should not really have been surprised that when I went to retrieve it, someone had stolen it. My mother was so frustrated with my lack of responsibility that she prevented me from replacing it. In the circumstances, and despite knowing that she would have refused me permission, hitch-hiking seemed to be the best option to enable me to have a good social life in Brighton.

~

Chapter 6 – An Alternative to High School

As soon as I returned home after leaving the Swiss school in mid-term just before my fifteenth birthday, the biggest question was where I would attend school. Roedean decided that if I returned I would only be able to study the few subjects I had been able to study at the Swiss school, which would have made it extremely difficult for me to attain university entrance.

For the summer and fall terms I was enrolled at a small local Brighton private girls' school with no high school classes. Unfortunately that autumn my nasal allergies worsened again, and when I had to miss school to go to London to see the specialist, I was so upset I announced that if this was going to be a regular occurrence for me to miss school for medical appointments and treatments then I would quit school. Either that or, since my parents were determined I go to university, I would stay home with my mother and study.

So it was that in January 1962 aged fifteen, I started attending a tutorial college in London which my sister had attended to "cram" for the retake of an important exam. Instead of attending high school, I took English, History, French and Latin in two-hour individual sessions with a tutor per week, eight hours total per week for the next two years. The college offered no more than a small study room in the basement with a table for up to six students and nothing else, so aside from those eight hours I studied mostly on my own at home or in a public library. During those two years I kept taking exams every few months, constantly inching me towards university.

At that time, my mother had a two-bedroom flat in London's Swiss Cottage where we both spent each week, returning to Lattenbells for the weekends. Sometimes she accommodated as many as six family members or friends in the flat for months at a time. At those times I slept on a murphy pull-out bed in the living-room, with no personal space of my own. The walls of the second bedroom, previously occupied by my brother, were lined with his books, and when only my mother and I were in the flat I was lucky enough to use that room. Those books taught me that the more I read the more interesting I found life to be. Many of the books were about his chosen subject, psychology, and others were serious fiction or such literary greats as Shakespeare and Chaucer. I became fascinated by such concepts as the hidden humanity of criminals, even including serious sex offenders, or the signals indicating how determined is a suicidal person or whether their actions are more in the form of an emotional cry for help. My weekdays involved long lonely hours of study, interspersed with this reading for my own enlightenment. I had no social life except with my mother and her friends.

My weekends at home in Ditchling on the other hand, with the Smugglers Snuff every Friday, were a social teenager's paradise.

A Memoir by Madeleine King

At the end of my two years at the London tutorial college I had scraped together just enough exams to get into university. As a teenager I had discussed my future career with my family, since my father thought I should have a profession in case my future husband died when I was forty and left me with six children to support! I presented them with my preferred options of becoming an air hostess, a model, or a secretary. Each one was met with significant criticism, so it was clear I had to come up with something more acceptable to them. One day after a visit from an eminent barrister friend of theirs I suggested maybe that would be a good career for me. The idea of becoming a courtroom lawyer like the television star Perry Mason seemed quite glamorous. My suggestion was met with great enthusiasm, and so for the time being at least, my future was decided. That same barrister advised against my doing a law degree as he considered studying another subject at the undergraduate level provided a broader education.

My history tutor had recommended me to the history department at a small college of the University of London where her husband headed the department, the School of Slavonic and East European Studies, and I accepted with gratitude. Three of my four grandparents, of whom I knew only one, had come to England from Russia and Eastern Europe as Jewish immigrants. This meant my family had a sense of connection to the history of this area.

The alternative placement was Sussex University just outside Brighton, but I turned down that opportunity when it became clear I

Expulsion

would only be offered a place because my father was on the university senate. At this stage in my education I felt as if I had lost the privilege of studying the subjects I loved and so it no longer mattered to me what I studied as long as I could fulfill my parents' wishes and get my education completed. My plan was to satisfy my parents by getting a degree by my twenty-first birthday and to satisfy my own dreams by getting married immediately afterwards and being a stay-at-home mum with six children.

~

Chapter 7 – Studying at the Sorbonne in Paris

Before starting at university, I spent the spring studying "Civilisation Francaise" at the Sorbonne in Paris. The French President, General de Gaulle had decided that the Sorbonne should develop a four-month course for future leaders from all over the world to study French history and culture from the very best professors France could offer, so that when those young people became people of influence back in their own countries they would understand France's viewpoints and think kindly of the country. The teaching was superb, but the learning conditions were dreadful so that the student riots that took place in 1968 protesting similar conditions were not at all surprising.

While in Paris I lived at 22 Rue Monsieur Le Prince located between Boulevards St. Michel and St. Germain in the heart of the Latin Quarter. Behind a huge solid gate preventing any view from the street, lay a typical cobbled courtyard surrounded by classical old apartment buildings. The ever-watchful concierge was housed immediately to the left on entering the courtyard, and she demanded a greeting on every entry and exit. My mother's schoolfriend Sylvia and her two daughters lived in a beautiful two-bedroomed apartment on the second floor, where I shared meals with the family and was always

Expulsion

made to feel welcome. My sleeping accommodation was on the top floor under the gables, originally used for servants. It was not possible to stand upright in my room because of the sloping roof, but it did have a large angled dormer window with a glorious view over the rooftops. There were three or four other rooms opening off the unlit narrow corridor, all occupied by local working people.

The only toilet which was shared by the top floor residents was a hole in the floor with stand-up foot pads. The tiny room had a solid door and no window and was pitch dark except for a single bare light on a timer, activated by a switch on the landing at the top of the staircase. Hence my times in that toilet were always fraught with anxiety lest I needed longer time than that permitted by the light. Sometimes I would finish in total darkness, fumbling to complete the task, and other times I would take the chance and run out to the light switch in the desperate hope that none of the other residents would be there to see me! I definitely needed all the English "stiff upper lip" I had learned at Roedean to cope with that toilet.

Sylvia was a warm and welcoming host. She was an artist who was then experimenting with playwriting. Although Sylvia had grown up in London with my mother, she had married a French artist with whom she lived in Tahiti until he left her for a local seventeen-year-old, when she went with the girls to Manhattan for ten years, before moving to Paris. She was an indulgent parent to her daughters, who were four and six years younger than me. She had huge difficulty setting boundaries, and even more difficulty enforcing them.

I was grateful to Sylvia for having me as a guest in her home, but I found the contrast between my mother's well-ordered life, now that she was more settled, and Sylvia's creative unpredictability difficult to admire. Possibly because of the instability of my early childhood, I had grown to respect and trust my mother above all others. Added to this, my mother had always encouraged me to develop and express my views on almost any subject I could name. These factors meant that I was not as loving and supportive a guest as I should have been.

From the apartment it was only a five-minute walk to the Sorbonne. I mentioned earlier how good the professors were and how bad the conditions. Monday mornings were our main time for lectures. About one thousand of us crammed into the stunning historic amphitheatre with tiered benches rising like the sun's rays from the lecturer's dais. We started at eight o'clock in the morning and if you did not arrive early you had to sit on the hard steps emanating outward from the dais for the rest of the morning. No-one worried about keeping these pathways clear in case of fire. Indeed, whenever the lecturer was especially popular, students would even huddle together sitting on the platform, literally at the professor's feet. Each lecture lasted one hour and every Monday morning we had to sit through five lectures in a row, right until one o-clock.

If we had arrived early those five hours were spent sitting on wooden benches with as many students as possible squeezed into each row. Not only was there no break scheduled during the morning and no cafeteria, but if you needed a bathroom break no-one would save your seat, forcing you to spend the remaining hours squished in between others on the steps.

My favourite lectures were those on French art. What I learned there has been my constant companion ever since; naturally, a love of the Impressionists but also an appreciation of the significance of many other artists from different centuries such as David and Watteau.

Once a week we had tutorials in groups of about eight students. My tutor had a forceful personality and much of her teaching has also stayed with me to this day. Her harshness was sometimes stunning. During one class she asked us what French dish we had learned to cook. I knew she loved a dish called "Blanquette de Veau" and having just eaten it prepared by Sylvia, I answered with that dish. As anticipated my response caused her to break into a warm smile of appreciation. Then she asked me to detail how to cook it. Recalling what Sylvia had taught me I described the making of the sauce. Start by making a roux by mixing butter and flour. "*What!*" she exclaimed horrified "*Never! It must be made with cream. Only peasants cook it with flour!*" I was shocked by the insult to Sylvia's excellent cooking.

Another time she enquired as to the style of furniture where each of us was staying. Louis XVI was particularly acceptable. When it came my turn and I had to tell her the furniture was modern she was appalled, implying that no self-respecting person would choose anything other than French antique furniture from the Classical period. After the Easter break one of the boys told her his parents had come to visit. In front of the whole class she quizzed him about the restaurant his father had chosen, the food ordered and the specific choice of wine; she then pronounced that his father was clearly a man of good taste. I was shocked that she felt she had the right to judge the parent of a student and to do it so publicly. She taught us Parisian social etiquette so that for example we would know not to telephone someone without first writing to ask permission to telephone them. And of course, how to write thank-you letters acceptable to French hosts.

Through her I had my first experience of feeling prejudiced against – not only because of her opinion of Sylvia's choices but also because of my own family. She expressed her view that the most favoured in the world were those who were born and had stayed in Paris. She then listed downward the various levels of humanity, ending with the lowest level being people like my family who she described as "deracine" or uprooted. It was a tough pill to swallow at that time, but in later years I came to believe she was totally mistaken; the most courageous were those who uprooted in order to improve their family's lot in life.

During the months in Paris I also felt that eligible young Frenchmen were likely to limit their interest in me to an amusing flirtation rather than a serious relationship because my involvement in their lives was of such short duration and I was from a different culture. The experience taught me something about being an outsider, someone perceived to have limited value.

Expulsion

Sadly, this was a time when the "white slave trade" was strongly in evidence in Paris. Girls would go out for a drink with a boy, consume the drink which had secretly been spiked with drugs, and would wake up having been transported to North Africa, where they were forced into addiction so they could be sold into a life of sexual slavery. Several girls disappeared in this way, and the Sorbonne and Alliance Francaise issued official warnings insisting we be on our guard and cautious at all times.

I received invitations from just one "bourgeois" family living (with the correct furniture) in the smart banking district near the Arc de Triomphe. It was a family with two sons of a suitable age who I and my family 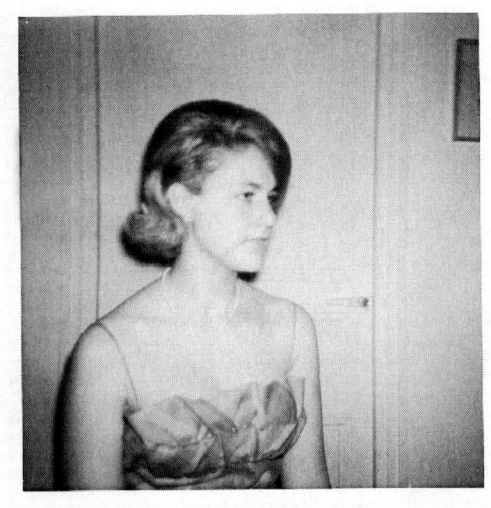 had met during a previous summer holiday on Lake Constance. The first time I went there I was very intimidated with all their uniformed staff, so different from my informal life in the Latin Quarter. The evening meal was served by a gloved attendant. I was the first one offered the silver casserole dish. It was an omelette. I had no idea what the meal would consist of or how much of the omelette I should take, so I took a small portion. The family asked kindly if that was enough for me. I declined their invitation to take more, waiting to find out what might come next. After we all finished our omelettes, those plates were replaced with fresh ones and once again I was the first one to be offered the new silver dish. What would it be? I lifted the lid with anticipation only to discover it was peas. Green peas. Nothing else. That was to be the full extent of our meal!

On another visit, after spending some time with the boys, the time came for me to change into a nice dress since they were taking me to a party in the Bois de Boulogne. They suggested I change my clothes in the small ballroom in their apartment. Alone in the room, at the very moment I had taken off my clothes and was standing in the middle of the room almost naked, the door opened at the far end and their father looked in. His apology did nothing to prevent my extreme embarrassment and my belief that his action was premeditated. After that I never visited them again.

While in Paris I felt full of life and energy. From morning to night I roamed the city, exploring every sort of cultural offering, especially art galleries and museums, avant-garde films and plays. I was never bored.

For the final exam at the Sorbonne I had to write a three-hour essay in French on the importance of Proust in the domain of psychology. Unfortunately, I had never read any of Proust's work. My lack of knowledge did not stop me writing the essay, inventing ideas as I wrote. As a result, I thought I was unlikely to pass the exam and get my diploma.

Expulsion

My German friend was returning home and asked me to collect her certificate of attendance and send it to her. She had reported that my name was not on the list of those who had succeeded. After I waited in the line-up for a very long time I decided I might as well request my own diploma at the same time; I did so with little hope having been told my name was not on the list. Nevertheless, I received my certificate and it said that I had been granted the diploma. To this day I have no idea whether I had really earned it or whether it was an administrative error!

There at the Sorbonne I had learned how Britain-centric my school history lessons had been, and how fascinating European history really was. This understanding stood me in good stead for my forthcoming undergraduate studies in European history.

Revisiting the Sorbonne in 2018

~

Chapter 8 - My Spiritual Awakening

As a student in Paris I spent a lot of time by myself with plenty of opportunity to consider the deeper questions of life.

My parents had both been born into Jewish families. My father's family had deep roots in the liberal Jewish community of Brighton and nearby Hastings, but he had been unable, as he told me, to find God and so was an atheist. He was a socialist who believed that no religion held relevance in the modern age, and that no parent had the right to impose their own religion on their children. By the time I was in Paris he had recently married Renie, a lovely Jewish widow who subsequently became the first patron of the now-famous annual Brighton Festival. With Renie by his side my father was able to rejoin the local Jewish community and rediscover pleasure participating in Jewish rituals.

My mother's parents immigrated to England in about 1900 from Russia and Poland, both speaking Yiddish as their first language. My grandfather died very young leaving my grandmother as a hard-working dressmaker and shop owner managing to make enough money to send all her five children to private schools. She was determined her children would be truly anglicized and leave behind the painful experiences of the ghettoes of Eastern Europe. For this reason she changed the family name from Leveson to the more English Lawson. Despite that, and several of her children marrying non-Jews, she definitely showed a preference for being amongst Jewish people throughout her life.

When my parents were first married and living in the village of Ditchling, my father angered the villagers by trying to buy up the fields surrounding the beautiful old village for housing development. This coupled with his well-known socialism brought out anti-Semitic attitudes in many of the mainly Conservative villagers. My mother found this hard to bear and, wanting a different future for us children, she changed our family name from Cohen to the more English Coleman.

As a young child I was already someone who worried about the deeper questions of life although I knew nothing of all of this. For example, my mother had to intervene with my teachers when I was seven because I was extremely concerned with simultaneously learning about Adam and Eve on the one hand and Darwin's Origin of the Species on the other.

At the invitation of a school friend when I was about ten years old I attended a Christian camp for a glorious week in the English Lake District. During that week I had my first encounter with God. It happened while I was sitting on the toilet praying that the doctor would not hurt me too much when he removed my septic splinter. My prayer felt heard by God so that I was more peaceful knowing that my suffering was in his hands. At the surgery the doctor scared me by picking up the sharpest of all his knives, but his cut near the inflammation was mercifully brief, and after that he told me the splinter would work its way out on its own.

I did stop to thank my new-found God, and have felt blessed by that sense of reliance on God ever since.

One day soon after that, my mother and I were walking into the village from Lattenbells when I described to her my own religious belief. She expressed great pleasure in my description and said that it matched the Unitarian faith which she liked very much, and of which there was a meeting place for worship nearby. I have warm memories of the Unitarian services we attended in the years that followed.

As a young teenager at Roedean I was profoundly moved by the beauty of the Church of England services and the obvious piety and faithfulness of the headmistress. When I asked my mother for permission to get baptized so I could be confirmed along with my school friends, she refused. She was critical of the Catholic Church's reaction to the Holocaust, and to the Protestant Churches' tolerant attitude to Apartheid while we were living in South Africa. Her reasoning for refusal was that I was at a very impressionable age in which it was unwise to make major life decisions which should await my greater maturity on reaching twenty-one.

During my time at school in Switzerland I attended local Protestant churches but craved the more formal Anglican rituals.

So it was that in Paris I took the opportunity to experience the Catholic Church. I began attending weekly mass alone at the nearby St. Sulpice church.

Whether through the connection with St. Sulpice or through the Sorbonne, I signed up to participate in a walking pilgrimage to Chartres Cathedral. On the appointed day thousands of us students arrived at a train station to start our journey. I was supremely ill-equipped, especially my footwear which was a pair of calf-length fashion boots. We walked all day, in some sort of formation even if a bit ragged, with priests heading up each section of fifty or so students. Sometimes we sang hymns, sometimes we were bidden to be silent and other times we chatted merrily. That night my group slept in a farmer's hay barns, lying on the floor or on the hay as best we could.

During the following morning we first saw the taller of the two famous spires of Chartres Cathedral visible as it peeped up over the horizon. We hoped this sighting meant it would not be too long before we arrived. In fact we had hours and hours still to trudge along. The weather was very warm. Several girls collapsed and had to be carried off by the hovering first aid personnel. Many like me were suffering dreadfully from inappropriate footwear.

When we reached the glorious cathedral that evening I marvelled both at my physical salvation as well as at the beauty of its blue stained-glass windows and the spiritual joy of completing this pilgrimage.

Expulsion

Despite my spiritual awakening, a few weeks later while I was worshipping at St. Sulpice, my attention became fixed on the ornate gold and silver objects around the altar and I became suddenly aware of the contradiction between what I was now experiencing and the biblical injunction against the worship of graven images. It was a thought that haunted me and prevented me from continuing to attend weekly mass.

After that it was many years before I again sought out and found a spiritual home.

~

Chapter 9 – Undergraduate Years

During my first year of university I continued to live at home with my mother, with weekdays in the London flat and weekends at Lattenbells. I drove her crazy since I left home early each morning and returned on the last tube train each night after playing cards, darts or snooker with my new-found friends. Through playing those games and ping-pong, at which I excelled, I met my first university boyfriend, Gordon. He was a year ahead, studying Russian Language and Literature, and was president of the students' union at college. He persuaded me to run for election as our representative for the National Union of Students, successfully coaching me through my first election campaign. I did attend a national conference but remember little about it except that I was in way over my head.

At the same time Harold Wilson, the first left-wing Prime Minister for thirteen years, appointed my father to the House of Lords as his key housing expert. He became Brighton's first-ever lord, Lord Cohen of Brighton. It was a great honour and it made me feel even more proud of his achievements.

Such titles were not to add to the aristocracy, being merely titles for life, but anachronistically it did still confer on me and my brother and

Expulsion

sister the title of "Honourable". It was fun to use it for a few years, especially as it definitely improved the service I received, but all three of us subsequently abandoned using the titles as they did not fit with our lifestyles.

My own undergraduate studies were focused on the political, geographic, philosophical, and economic history of each of the countries then included in the Soviet Union east of East Germany. The college specialized in research on Russia and its dependant countries and paid little attention to the quality of its teaching for undergraduates.

My professor of the history of political thought was a Hungarian refugee who had escaped his country during the revolution of 1956 when the country was invaded by the Russian communists. I learned so much from his vigorous debates about the perils of communism and the duty to uphold democracy even when it involved taking up arms.

At the start of my second year, my Brighton school friend Carty and I rented a basement flat in London's Maida Vale. Having left school at sixteen she was now working for a literary agency representing authors in their negotiations with publishers. She soon fell in love with my cousin's best friend. Sadly, a few weeks before they were to be married, he broke her heart, suddenly dumping her. For a full week she starved herself, and never managed to eat normally again. After many months of wasting away so that she was dangerously thin, she was admitted as an inpatient suffering from anorexia to England's leading mental hospital, the Maudsley.

Amongst our many friends I was the only one who visited Carty in hospital. Sometimes she could not recognize me because the drugs they were giving her were so strong. That was scary. She was in a small group situation with about six other long-term patients suffering from both anorexia and bulimia, who I got to know a little. After a few visits, on my arrival at the hospital one day, I was asked unexpectedly if I would take Carty out for a visit. We went to the trendy Kings Road in Chelsea; she was so high with excitement and drugs that it was challenging for me to have any control over her at all. When we crossed the busy road I could not tell from one minute to the next whether she would continue in the same direction or turn around and head back or do a pretty twirl in the middle of traffic; she was overwhelmed with the excitement of it all.

The next time I arrived for a visit the nurse in charge requested I take all the patients out with Carty. I was stunned with her request; I had to come to terms with the fact she considered me such a responsible person; what would Madame Palisch have said! The patients absolutely loved our expedition, and it became the first of several. Each time I knew how close we all were to disaster, but I knew if I said no then they would have no more outings.

On one occasion I told them I could empathize with their mental health issues. One of them shocked me by pronouncing there was no way I would ever end up in their situation. The others joined in,

Expulsion

explaining their view that the world was divided into those who might cross the line into unwellness and those who would not – and I was firmly on the side of those whose strength will always keep them whole.

When Carty was finally released, there was nowhere for her to go, except her parents' home where she quickly deteriorated. I was so upset that I became keen to assist other young people recovering from addictions and mental health issues, which I was eventually able to do through working with the head of a specialized hospital unit, and establishing a fund to support those making their way back into the world.

During that same year I too fell in love and got engaged to be married. My brother and sister had both recently married, and I was keen to follow in their footsteps. Peter was a brilliant final year student in Russian Language and Literature from Yorkshire in the north of England, with whom I had a very tumultuous relationship, powerful but painful.

Following his graduation, we travelled in Yugoslavia and Greece. During our time on a Greek island that baking hot August I read three Dostoyevsky novels, about fifteen hundred pages of dense literature! Not something I would have expected of myself as a very social twenty-year-old on a romantic holiday with her beloved fiancée. During the return journey I watched with envy a girl laughing joyously with her friends, and recalled times before I had fallen in love, when that girl might have been me. I realized then that the relationship was not a happy one, and I called off the engagement.

~

Chapter 10 – My Tumultuous Year

I was so devastated by the ending of my relationship with my fiancée Peter that my whole body felt as if it would collapse at any moment. My sister did her best to support me, letting me know that all I had to do was survive the hour at hand, and then the next one, until eventually I could function again.

I was soon thrust into the raft of challenges that fall would bring my way. My father became deathly ill after suffering from leukemia for several years. He was well-known nationally by then and among his many attributes he had been known as very athletic and energetic. At sixty-nine years of age he did not want to be seen in his weakened state. In the circumstances his move to the Royal Marsden Hospital in London, England's foremost cancer hospital, was done in secret. As an undergraduate with many friends who I needed especially at that time, it was tough to keep his and my family's suffering private. I was told that he was relieved that my engagement had ended since he had been genuinely concerned about the unsuitability of our relationship; so much so that he had hired a personal detective to keep track of our movements and friendships. In one way he was absolutely right to have been concerned; I was the start of a generational social change, and before learning about the availability of the new pill and other family planning alternatives, I had nearly got pregnant.

Adding to this trauma, when I visited him in hospital, I upset him by telling him my engagement was back on again after the previous break-up in Greece. He let me know how disappointed in me he was and so anxious for my future. After my visit, during his final days, he wrote farewell letters to my brother and sister. I was devastated to learn later that he had decided I was too immature to receive one.

When it came to my father's funeral, my fiancée was unable to provide me any emotional support, because he could not turn his attention away from his own fragile ego. For me that was the last straw and I finally had the courage to bring the relationship to a complete end.

With all this emotional turmoil I was unable to concentrate on my studies. My sister arranged for me to spend a few weeks living and working in a mission house in a poor south London neighbourhood. The building and its occupants were similar to that portrayed in the television series "Call the Midwife" with a Church of England minister but no nuns, and our focus was the general welfare of those in the neighbourhood rather than their health. The food and conversation at meals with the other live-in staff were unimaginably dull, but my work was to help run a pre- and post-school daycare for latch-key kids. It was eye-opening work since I had no previous experience of such kids. Their every second word was a swear word worse than any I had ever encountered. But my leader taught me to be patient and forgiving since they were only learning from the behaviour of their parents, and ours was not to judge, but to offer them a safe environment where they could explore their creativity to the extent it did not harm anyone else. It was my first experience of serving others – and I cherished every moment.

On top of everything else happening to me, my family doctor decided that I needed to undergo exploratory surgery for gastro-intestinal issues. I was scared and the family doctor did not help by explaining that if when I awoke after surgery I found tubes coming out of me it would signify they had found something serious, but if they did not find anything too bad, they would probably have removed my appendix for good measure (which was what happened). My post-operative wound felt worse every day, but the hospital staff determined I was a hypochondriac and a malingerer - and they sent me home.

A few days later the wound opened - and my innards were visible to the naked eye! I was horrified at the sight and very scared. Luckily, my brother-in-law who was a doctor and was staying with us over the Christmas holiday, was able to keep the wound dressed and healing on a daily basis. The intimacy involved was very embarrassing with the wound being below my bikini line and my being alone with him each time with me lying on my bed.

After that experience of having been disbelieved by the hospital doctors and nurses, I determined to learn to be a better patient so in future doctors would trust what I was telling them; never again did I want my symptoms to be so disparaged.

In January at my follow-up medical appointment, the surgeon said that I was too weak to return to attending university classes and insisted I needed more rest and would have to take time off from my studies. His recommendation involved delaying my graduation from university until the summer of the following year.

I was horrified. By then I desperately wanted to be done with that small college and that stage of my life as soon as possible. My father's death coupled with my failed engagement contributed to my sense of needing to "get out of there". I decided I would prove the surgeon wrong and would graduate with my B.A. Honours that July.

In order to do so I wrote out a detailed calendar for the following six months, dividing every day into study periods, eating times, relaxation and sleep – and I stuck to its every detail.

During those months I would take the Tube train every morning to the British Museum, where under the central dome of the building lay the magnificent Reading Room. Since English language books on some periods of Eastern European history were virtually impossible to find elsewhere, I had obtained the rarely granted opportunity of studying there. Only privileged researchers who could not access their sources anywhere else in England could obtain entry. I was possibly the only undergraduate with such privilege and was lucky enough to make friends with many brilliant researchers. Each person had a leather

Expulsion

Photo courtesy British Museum blog

topped ample desk space along a row of about six or eight. Each row fanned out from the central information desk like rays from the sun. The wood was beautiful and above all was the magnificent cupola.

In order to get books, you filled in a form for each one and it was hand delivered to your desk. Sometimes my desk was littered with more than ten heavy tomes at a time. I was like a kid in a candy store.

A Memoir by Madeleine King

Request for "Foreign Office List for 1876"
for M. Coleman
[Discovered by chance between the pages of "The Brothers
Karamazov" during the writing of this memoir.]

One of my exams would be a piece of Russian prose which I was to translate into English. Despite some effort on my part, I had not been very successful in learning Russian. I had thoroughly enjoyed spending two summers in Cambridge studying the language, but I suspect it was the pleasure of being in that beautiful city as well as having a wonderful social time that made it so pleasurable. In the event I cannot remember spending much timing studying. However I was not worried at the possibility of failing the Russian exam because I believed that they could not afford to fail me. How did I reach such a conclusion? It was because as a student representative I had been asked to address the funding body for the university and had told them that the college had not provided me, or any other student, with sufficient learning opportunities in Russian language. As a direct result they had changed the curriculum for future students to ensure they had adequate teaching. I was determined to try my luck in the Russian exam by only translating the first two words, and then walking out. I believed my lack of preparedness was their issue not mine, and so they should not fail me.

When it came to the final exams, the format was totally brutal; over a period of five days I had to have memorized one thousand years of the histories of each of the countries of Russia and Eastern Europe. There was no access to materials and limited choice of which question to answer. The timing was so precise that each minute had to be taken up with writing (with an ink pen in long hand) with absolutely no time for reflection. The results from these exams were the only factor in our graduating scores – nothing was added by way of class participation, mid-terms, or any other written work during our three years of study.

Several of my colleagues were overcome with the stress – and after that it would only be possible for them to achieve the lowest passing grade, however competent they were, on retaking the exams that September or the following summer. And at that time in England your grade would determine how far you could ever get in your future career. Scary in the extreme!

My grade was in the mid-range, as good as I had hoped for given how much I had missed of my final year. It was a grade that prevented me from pursuing a desired level of entry to the diplomatic corps and was therefore life-altering; but that was something I had had to take into consideration when making the decision to attempt to graduate that year. The one great life-long intellectual benefit of being forced to retain all those facts for the exams was that at long last I grasped the inter-connectivity of those facts and could appreciate the great movements of European history.

The only way I survived the experience of that week was with a sense of total discipline. For example, I had to stop myself from running to catch a bus or cross a road because the extra exertion would cause me to get into panic-mode. I did graduate successfully and felt hugely proud of my achievement. In fact, that year I was the only student to graduate from the three-year course.

My sense of pride in the self-discipline I exhibited made me feel like an elite athlete; once I knew I could set goals and hold myself to account and work to achieve exactly what I wanted – and get there successfully – wow, was it ever life-changing!

My confidence in myself was also strengthened by coming to terms with how much pleasure it gave me to be able to help others; that ability was like a God-given gift to be treasured for the rest of my life.

But Madame Palisch had not been entirely wrong – I loved to party and could easily lead a group into having fun and challenging established norms. And she certainly was not the last person in authority to regret the day I arrived in their space.

~

Chapter 11 – Losing My Direction

Exams completed, it was time for beautifying myself in preparation for my twenty-first birthday celebration at London's Savoy Hotel. Two days later on the flight to the gorgeous Mediterranean island of Majorca my mother kindly handed me a bottle of slimming pills which I dutifully started taking as per the instructions on the bottle. After an entertaining evening with other family members all staying at a luxury hotel, I was so lively there was no way I could sleep. There came a time in the evening when it was clear everyone wanted to retire to bed, but I was so enthusiastic that I found it hard to let them go. Sharing a room with my mother I was so fearful of waking her that I spent the night sitting in the empty bathtub of our bathroom, thoroughly uncomfortable but happy to have a book to read. The following morning when I suggested I might need to take fewer pills per day, she was horrified that I had been overdosing because this pill bottle into which she had transferred the pills had instructions for a totally different prescription!

My party at the Savoy Hotel was a wonderful event with about sixty guests for a sit-down dinner, followed by an influx of about fifty more of my friends for dancing and dessert and a "breakfast" snack served at one in the morning. The girls looked fabulous in their pretty dresses and the band was great at keeping nearly everyone dancing until the early hours of the morning. Many of my male friends had never worn dinner jackets nor attended a function at the Savoy. One of the boys told me it was an expensive evening for him since he, being unused to seeing an attendant in the washroom, felt obliged to tip him every time he used the facilities.

My date for the evening was a playwright who I had met while studying at the Reading Room of the British Museum, remembered by me now only by his first name Ed. I had told him of a vivid dream I had, set against a surreal version of my father's death. With my permission he turned that dream into a stage play, and I subsequently had the experience of seeing it performed at the Round House in London's Chalk Farm, where it was performed as one of his three short plays. The only comment I heard from other theatregoers was that the one based on my dream was the only one of the three to show true originality. I felt privileged to see my dream performed, but I found the experience quite unnerving, having my private fantasy dissected by strangers. Shortly afterwards I lost touch with the playwright and had no way of knowing if my dream was ever performed again.

After university I knew the next step was supposed to be my studying to become a barrister. But I did not have the courage to go the few blocks from my college to sign up. None of my friends were following that path of further education let alone legal education. My university college had no career assistance whatsoever, my powerful and connected father had just died and my mother, having never worked outside the home, was unable to help.

I had no idea which direction to follow.

I got a management trainee job in computer programming with NCR, the only company that even gave me an interview. Six months later I came to understand how the glass ceiling would limit my career aspirations, when a regional manager, asking me which of my colleagues was likely to be his future boss, laughed at my questioning why it might not be me. He then explained that the only path to management was through the experience of being a salesman, and there never had been a female salesman, a situation he could not imagine being changed. At the same time I did not appreciate staff like me having to use only the back door as our entrance and having to literally clock in every day. Since I was clearly ill-prepared and unsuited for life as a junior cog in a big corporation, I left that job.

That spring I went with a boyfriend in his beautiful old MGA to visit "behind the Iron Curtain". The car, named the "Beast" by me, was lovely to look at but was mechanically unreliable and provided virtually no room for luggage. First we made our way to Prague, where the people were celebrating what became known as Dubcek's Spring of 1968, immediately preceding the Russian invasion and the end of their new-found liberties. We loved the old city whose history impressed me with its adoption of an early version of Protestant beliefs accompanied by great national pride in confronting the combined forces of European Catholicism. I was also especially moved by visiting the old Jewish ghetto and attending an outdoor concert just outside the walls of the old castle. At that time Czechs were extremely limited in travel opportunities since they were only allowed to convert their currency into three British pounds per year. This meant that we were constantly harassed on the streets to change money on the black market. My anxiety about landing in jail there prevented us from accepting any such pleas.

The next stop in our journey was the medieval city of Cracow in southern Poland. Every day a trumpeter in ancient costume saluted each hour from the tower overlooking the main square with its cobbled pavement and ancient market stalls.

We were visiting my university friend who was there for graduate studies in Polish literature. He had requested I bring some dress fabric, two pairs of blue jeans and a bikini, which I did in the belief the items would be his gift to a new girlfriend. Some hours after I gave them to him, he surprised me by handing me large sums of Polish cash. He had sold them on the black market, and by forcing me to accept the money he was involving me in the very act of local criminality I had so strenuously avoided in Prague. With the money, which I was unable to persuade him to take back, we took him out to the only functioning restaurant. Since we would not have been permitted to leave Poland with the currency, we also purchased crystal glassware at one of the only stores just before departure, which I wedged between my feet for the journey home.

Expulsion

Our last visit was to Warsaw. I was fascinated by the fact the city had been completely rebuilt after the War, a new version of its old beauty. It was delightful to see, although its newness meant it had none of the authenticity of cities like Prague and Cracow. Our host had worked in London with my friend as a computer programmer for the Polish expanding automobile manufacturing industry. His family were very anti-communist, at least partly because their home had been partitioned so it could be shared with those moved in by the Party. No-one was permitted more floor space than deemed essential, a very tough situation.

I was surprised to hear the opinion of my hosts that it was incumbent on the Russian army to invade Czechoslovakia (as it then was) to prevent the spread of what they perceived as German expansionism. Their acceptance of their country's reliance on the Soviet Union was dependant on it continuing to protect them. They viewed the history of their country as being one alternating between domination from either Russia or Germany, with no possibility for their own independence. This conversation was in stark contrast to the views subsequently expressed in England, and it was a lifelong lesson about how very localized our media reporting is, and how valuable to consider how news might be perceived from the standpoint of other nationalities.

While staying in Warsaw I followed up with the wishes of an aunt in England who had requested I visit the sizeable city of Lodz to see if I could find any remnants of my extended family. In Poland whenever

I mentioned this quest I was saddened by the anti-Semitic views I encountered, even from my university friend.

In the MGA we drove to Lodz one day. Maps of the city were unobtainable because they might help an enemy, so we found the police station and examined the map pinned to the back on the entry door! From this I was able to navigate to the location of the former family pharmacy. Eventually through asking around I met up with a woman who thought we might have a family connection through her husband. We chatted together in halting French, our only common language. She had survived the War because she herself was not Jewish, and she was thrilled to meet me because not one member of her husband's family had survived the Holocaust. Her recounting the disappearances of all of them and every single other Jew in the city was horribly vivid. It was a meeting that brought home to me the enormity of what had happened.

Our return to London took us through the infamous Checkpoint Charlie in Berlin, where every centimetre of the MGA and its contents were very thoroughly examined by armed guards. My first twenty-four hours in west Berlin, heart of The West, made me feel like the proverbial kid in a candy store. However, in the days after that I came to wonder about our focus in the "free" West on consumerism, in stark contrast to the pleasurable more organic and local lifestyles of our hosts in Poland and Prague.

Once back in London I was plunged into a low state, with no structure in my life and no certainty of direction. Eventually I reached out to

Expulsion

my sister in a long telephone conversation. She persuaded me that if I had a profession I would find myself more engaged through my work as well as being less subject to the glass ceiling so prevalent in the business world.

~

Chapter 12 – Becoming an English Barrister

With guidance from my sister I dredged up the courage to enrol for a three-year course as a Bar student preparing to become a barrister at a professional London college. I had not wanted to become a full-time student again but surprised myself by falling in love with the study of law, and my new colleagues eventually became good friends. My spending long hours studying was balanced by my wish to chart a new course in my social life. My undergraduate years had taken me away from my Brighton friends, and I also moved away from my university friends in becoming a law student. Through a flat-sharing agency I shared a flat with four girls for a couple years, but when they all fell in love and I was still on my own, the situation made me miserable and I left to live on my own.

My classmates, all studying identical subjects leading to the annual Bar exams, were a good mix; with some having employment experience but no university education while others had degrees from universities including Oxford and Cambridge. Amazingly my classmates included a past president of the United Nations, and a retired CEO of Shell Northern Ireland who had always dreamed of being a barrister. There were also some on judicial scholarships from

Expulsion

countries such as Malaysia who would become senior judges in their countries on successful completion of our course.

In the year-end exams we were in competition with others throughout England and Wales and many Commonwealth countries taking the professional exams to become barristers-at-law. The solicitors' exams were entirely separate; barristers at that time being considered the senior branch since only they were eligible to become judges.

At the end of my first year I stunned everyone including myself by outperforming all my classmates and placing fifth nationally (and internationally). The results were published in the Times newspaper. At about midnight the night before, I drove from my home in Notting Hill Gate to Fleet Street where the paper was printed so I could pick up an early copy. I was so thrilled by seeing my name in the top twelve entrants that my leg cramped up on the return journey through London's bustling West End, and I had to do an emergency stop in the middle of the street. Luckily, I had not caused an accident as it was late at night, so the streets were not busy as in the daytime.

My second-year results were less good owing to a broken heart, caused when my boyfriend who I was crazy about, unceremoniously dumped me during a weekend visit with his parents just a couple of weeks before the exams. Thankfully, my mother came to my rescue, letting me stay at her London house while she plied me with regular quantities of Scotch whisky whenever I awoke from dreaming that I had slept through the exams, escaping them altogether.

For my final year I had fully recovered so that, when competition in the exams included all those with an LLB law degree, I placed thirteenth overall in England, Wales and the Commonwealth. A friend sent me a telegram saying: "per ardua ad astra" which translates as "through hard work to the stars". I felt immensely proud. Above all else I would have loved to share the news with my late father and delight in his astonishment and pride.

During the following summer I had the opportunity to work in the law firm of a friend of my parents. The law firm comprised the owner, a solicitor of thirty years' experience and his junior partner with five years' experience plus a couple of support staff. It was located in a poor area of south London, where the majority of clients were on welfare which normally entitled them to Legal Aid. The work was mostly family law, criminal defence, landlord and tenant, small contract disputes and employment issues. Much of my time was spent filling out Legal Aid forms on behalf of clients, which involved questioning them on the minutiae of their lives to confirm they met the means test. I was dismayed at this intrusion which gave me an incredible insight into the realities of life for large numbers of the population. It felt to me a real privilege to be useful to them. I came to believe that if I had been born into their families I would have acted in similar ways to them. When young male clients repeatedly stole car parts so they could play at being mechanics, I empathized with their lack of contrition since society was showing no encouragement in enabling them to find a better future. When young women with low self esteem found themselves trapped in disastrous marriages forced on them by societal norms because of unwanted pregnancies, my heart went out to them. When adults who had grown up in families entirely dependant financially on welfare, found themselves unable to summon the discipline to survive paid employment, I could only seek to comprehend their daily challenges.

The firm's owner believed that I had found my calling, and he urged me to quit pursuing a career as a barrister and transfer to that of solicitor so that I could remain with the firm permanently. While I did love my time in that law practice, I was uncertain that I would be satisfied spending my whole life there. Becoming a barrister was a path leading to far more career opportunities, not least of which was eventually becoming a judge.

By the time I finished my Bar exams I was eager to join the two thousand barristers then practising in London. Most common law barristers have their places of business, or "chambers", in an area of London known as the Temple, situated between the River Thames and Fleet Street. It is governed by the Inner and Middle Temples, two of the four Inns governing and educating the Bar (barristers) of England and Wales. The area, which surrounds the twelfth century Temple Church, is so named because it was occupied by the Knights Templar on their return from the Crusades.

In order to qualify as a barrister I was obliged to join an Inn, and I chose the Inner Temple, of which I am still a member. An unusual requirement is to eat a specified number of dinners in one's Inn, an odd rule dating back to the ancient times when students lived in the

Inns during their education. Dinners were served in the Inn's great old hall, with students and barristers sitting on wooden benches at long tables. Eating these dinners was seen as an opportunity to get to know other members of your Inn, whether fellow students, barristers, or judges, and whether they lived in London or came there from any part of the far-flung Commonwealth. Many years before my time Mahatma Gandhi had eaten his dinners too in the Inner Temple in preparation for his being called to the Bar.

The first major challenge after the exams was for me to find a barrister willing to give me the necessary twelve months as his barrister-in-training. My exam results were considered irrelevant in finding such an opening, since many barristers considered my success irrelevant because the standard was professionally rather than academically based.

Being a young woman without the right connections made it seem impossible to find a barrister willing to take me as a "pupil". Indeed even the "sponsor" allotted to me by the Inner Temple declared at our first meeting that he did not believe in women at the Bar, unless, as he put it they were *"either brilliant or beautiful"*. His attitude clearly showed that he considered I was neither.

It was my mother's outreach that succeeded in coming to my rescue. She had asked so many people she eventually somewhat unusually even asked her sister, my aunt Pearl. Her answer: *"In my block of flats there's an older lady I sometimes see in the lift and I think her son is a barrister. The next time she's in the lift with me I'll ask her."* It

Expulsion

turned out the son was not only a senior barrister but was also the elected head of about seventeen barristers, the most junior two of whom, having just completed their first five years, were eligible to take on their first pupils.

All members of the Bar had to practise from a set of chambers where each barrister was a "tenant", normally remaining in one set of chambers throughout their whole working lives. Each was obliged to be self-employed and have all their work flow to them through their shared clerk. The clerk, traditionally having started in chambers as a teenager, was in charge of all administrative and financial aspects on behalf of all members of chambers.

So by arrangement I made my way to the chambers at King's Bench Walk in the Temple, an ancient set of row houses frequently used as background in English period films.

Jeffrey agreed to be my Pupil Master for the first six months and Stanley the second. During those months, apart from learning how they did their job, I also contributed by way of acting as a research assistant for which privilege I did not receive any pay. Instead, I paid them a total of one hundred pounds or about one hundred sixty Canadian dollars.

At the start Jeffrey was very frosty which was especially unpleasant because I had to stick by his side through all our working hours; when meeting with clients, appearing in court, negotiating with opposing barristers, meeting with judges in private and even travelling to courts throughout England. Luckily, a wise old friend suggested to me that Jeffrey might be feeling defensive and so I should quit talking about myself or offering opinions and focus all my energy on building up his own ego. It was difficult for me to put his advice into action! However, it turned out to be brilliant advice and led to a close relationship with Jeffrey and a wonderful learning experience.

My time with Stanley was very different, partly because he was a genius who rarely relied on my research, and also because by then I was able to take my own cases, and they occupied most of my time.

Those first court cases taught me so much! My very first bail application was in a London magistrates' court. My client was a young man suspected of break-and-enter who had an extensive history of petty criminality. When my application for bail was granted, he was totally overjoyed at my success in winning him his temporary freedom. There were several factors making the whole experience especially confounding for me. On the one hand I was trying to show off my newfound professionalism, striving to appear as someone who knew what they were doing. I wanted to show that I could be relied on by a client at the their time of huge stress. On the other hand, this client had so much more experience of courtroom proceedings that I did. Nevertheless, he was delighted by my innocence of how bail applications actually worked. Between the two of us we got the job done, and each of us was thrilled.

In the years that followed, I was often in court every day of the working week. I enjoyed the adrenaline rush of a successful

Expulsion

courtroom outcome, which is a pleasurable release of extreme tension and concentration experienced by many barristers on completion of a case, and I understood how easy it is to become addicted to that special physical sensation.

~

Chapter 12 – A Woman Barrister in a Man's World

During the second six months of my pupillage, my attention turned to my getting a tenancy in those chambers. I was happy to be among its seventeen members as well as enjoying a very good relationship with the clerk and his staff.

One day that spring Stanley shocked me by explaining that my tenancy had been refused. I was devastated. I had wanted to stay in those chambers more than anything else in my life to that point. I had used every bit of tact and charm and intelligence I could muster around every single member during the previous couple of months, at the same time as winning a lot of cases and getting positive feedback on my written work and my relationship with solicitors on whom we relied for our work.

It emerged that I had been black balled by one member, using his personal veto. In the chambers' meeting he had said he would only agree to allowing in a second female if she were so brilliant they would be foolish to turn her away. In his view I did not measure up to that high standard.

Expulsion

I had developed the notion that if I wanted something enough, and worked hard enough to get it, then success would come my way. But now I was stymied in my career goal despite doing everything I could to achieve it. It was just one man who barred my path forward; one man who had always been courteous and friendly towards me. Later I was to find it was not uncommon for men who challenged women's career path to be those who were otherwise unfailingly courteous to them. A lesson I had had to learn the hard way.

I considered quitting the Bar at that point, but the clerk dissuaded me saying: *"If you could see how your face shines after a good day in court, you'd know you won't give up. You'll find a tenancy somewhere and you'll have a successful career at the Bar. I'll do my best to help you."*

Despite the rejection the work continued to flow in for me during the few weeks remaining for me at that set of chambers. One of my cases was a long jury trial at the Old Bailey where the biggest criminal cases took place. There were several defendants each of whom was represented by a QC (Queen's Counsel, a very senior barrister) and his junior, of which I was one. John Mortimer, the eminent playwright of Rumpole fame, was one of the QCs. The trial was so tedious as to be totally forgettable and over tea at Twining's in Fleet Street John Mortimer amused us by talking of his low boredom threshold which prevented him from staying awake during large parts of the proceedings.

The conversation then turned to a new piece of gossip. It was reported that a set of chambers had chosen to look for a female tenant, such an odd course to pursue. Naturally, I was intrigued. I ran all the way back to King's Bench Walk and asked the clerk to help me get it before someone else might beat me to it. Other heads of chambers had already turned me down, either because they did not consider me good enough or because, as they frankly told me, they did not believe in women at the Bar. The clerk did help me, and I was accepted without any further delay. My mother was enormously proud of me.

So it was that in the summer of 1972 when I was twenty-six years old, I began my law practice as a tenant of 6 Pump Court in the Temple, with my name painted on a board at the foot of the stone staircase along with the fourteen or so other members of chambers.

As previously described, all a barrister's work flows through the clerk. It turned out that Leslie, the senior clerk at this chambers ran everything with an iron fist, having been there for more than a quarter century. The head of chambers had decided to accept me as the second female while Leslie was away on vacation, believing this was the only way to avoid his objections. Leslie was so furious at what he considered to be this deception, that he spent the next two years, as he subsequently admitted to me, trying to "break" me. He had various ways to do this. For example, when a solicitor telephoned asking for me, Leslie would sometimes say that I was probably out somewhere having a manicure or shopping, despite Leslie knowing that I was in my room eagerly awaiting any paid work. On one occasion he sent me

Expulsion

to appear for a client in a faraway court necessitating a long train journey and other expenses for me, only to tell me later that he had waived payment for my work in exchange for a big trial bringing in a large fee for another member of chambers. He would give me the lowest paid work that had not been assigned to any particular barrister. He would accept appointments for me to appear in court during my previously scheduled holidays.

At the end of two years Leslie told me that I had successfully survived his manoeuvres, and that he had come to appreciate being my clerk.

Despite all of the challenges I loved the work, which I found wholly absorbing and which provided me a wide range of experiences day by day. Also I so enjoyed the mutual respect, sense of shared experience and camaraderie of fellow barristers. The fellowship was so strong that wherever I was in court in England, every other barrister accepted me as their instant colleague even when I was their courtroom opponent.

As a junior barrister my legal briefs detailing all aspects of the case would often be delivered to the clerk's room at about six in the evening for a court hearing commencing the following morning, whether it was a summary trial, divorce, or other case. This invariably meant not knowing until then whether I would need to work through the evening hours and even right through the night. The following morning, arriving at a courthouse was frequently the first time I met the client I would be representing in the courtroom proceedings. It was very scary for both me and for the client!

A Memoir by Madeleine King

On one occasion my brief was to represent a three-month old baby who the local authority claimed had been severely beaten about the skull by his parents, and they were requesting the court authorize taking the baby away from the parents. I had never been involved with such a case, and I worked through that night trying to understand how these things might happen. When I met the parents at court they denied harming their baby and they were devastated by the thought of losing him. They pleaded with me to defend them. I did my best for them and succeeded in preventing the local authority taking the baby into their care, despite the fact that I was deeply troubled that the baby was in danger of mistreatment by the parents. The barristers' accepted code of ethics was that it was the role of the court to decide right from wrong, and not that of a barrister to prejudge that decision. Sometimes this was a tough rule to follow in practice.

Another time my brief was to defend a university professor who had experienced a mental breakdown one evening during which time he behaved as if he had taken drugs and was hallucinating that a stranger's car which he broke into was in fact his own living room. I was horrified to discover his name was that of a close friend of my older sister's who was also a university professor. At the courthouse I was shown through to the jail part of the building, with heavy iron doors clanking closed behind me. Then the jailer opened the door to my client's cell and proceeded to lock the cell door behind me as soon as I stepped inside. The cell was about eight feet square with a hole in the middle of the floor for the prisoner to relieve himself. The place stank. My client was quite literally climbing the walls. Despite the fact he was in huge mental distress, a great weight was lifted off me as he was not the same professor as my sister's friend. Eventually after a number of court hearings the judge recognized that he was unlikely to reoffend and that his excellent academic career deserved to be preserved.

Once, when I met my client at the courthouse, he was furious that he had been given a female lawyer. Jimmy was extremely rude to me, but when he could see that the hearing was about to start, he agreed begrudgingly to have me represent him. He was seeking to overturn a conviction for assault while resisting arrest. His story was that in the early hours of the morning in London's theatre district he and a police constable had locked eyes with each other in such a way that the constable saw his stare as a challenge to fight him. Reacting to what the constable imagined as a threat, he arrested Jimmy without anything further having happened. It was Jimmy's physically resisting that arrest that caused the charge, but Jimmy maintained he was entitled to resist arrest since it was unlawful. Jimmy also alleged the constable fabricated a story about Jimmy's actions before the arrest because he knew he had merely reacted to Jimmy's hostile glare. Jimmy said it was a man's issue; that other men would understand, but not a woman. He was certainly right that I could not understand his defence, and I did not believe that the constable was lying. But our fundamental ethic at the Bar was that unless we were in possession of facts proving guilt, it was not for us to judge guilt or innocence but merely to do our best for the client. So, in that spirit I gave him the opportunity to explain to the male judges his version of events, and much to my amazement, they acquitted him on the spot.

A very scary experience happened one day when I was about to leave a courtroom having just finished a routine case, when the judge pointed to me and said that he was giving me a "dock brief". This was an ancient precursor to legal aid whereby a judge selected a barrister present in the courtroom and effectively ordered them to provide legal counsel to an accused presently in the dock for a tiny fixed fee. In this instance I am sure the judge gave it to me out of spite, either because he had not liked my presentation or because he did not approve of female barristers. As I sat there in court in my black robes and my barrister's wig I was immediately handed the papers concerning my new client. A chill went through me as I read about him. Dave was charged with violent assaults while serving a jail term for violence. The report from the prison authorities said that he showed no remorse and was a disruptive influence in jail. He was not supported by any family member since previously he had held his mother and sister captive in their homes and without proper heating during the winter months. On top of all that, he was a black man who demonstrated a violent hatred towards white people, especially females. I dreaded how he would react to having me represent him on that very day in his application to the judge to be freed on bail pending his trial.

He was being held in the cells attached to the courtroom, and it was clear I needed to see him and hear his version of events. The jailer led me to the cells. Choosing from a set of enormous keys he opened the

Expulsion

first door and then locked it behind us. Then I walked behind him along the narrow corridor with cells on either side. On reaching Dave's, cell the jailer opened the heavy door and ushered me in. He said I should shout and rattle the door when I wanted to get out. Then he locked me in, and I heard his footsteps retreating along the corridor and the main door being locked shut behind him. I was alone with my client. I was terrified, but I had to get on with the job.

Amazingly, Dave turned out to be very co-operative with me and seemed genuinely surprised to find that someone was actually prepared to help him. He told me he had been misunderstood by the prison authorities and that his mother and sister would be pleased to vouch for him and would travel the long distance from Liverpool to London to reassure the judge so long as I could get the bail application postponed. When I was finished with the interview it was Dave who assisted me to call for the jailer, rattling the door and getting help from other inmates. It was Dave who helped me; the man I had feared so much on entry to his cell, and with good reason on my part for that fear.

The experience of finding him to be co-operative and grateful made me question the assessment of him by those in authority. I wondered if too many of them had based their interactions with him on the basis of previous reports, without opening up to him and listening without prejudice. I was not so naïve as to ignore the fact that he had a lot to gain by winning my trust, and that he may in other circumstances have behaved just as badly as reported.

I may have been influenced by having received a bad but incorrect assessment of my own teenage self. That experience had shown me that if someone treated me as a potential troublemaker, I would not bother to disabuse them of that negative perception. Whereas when someone treated me with respect, I tried my hardest to earn that privilege.

Eventually the jailer showed up to let me out, and the judge reluctantly agreed to the postponement. A few weeks later I returned to the court for Dave's mother and sister to be present, and although I was almost as sceptical as everyone else, they did turn up and assure the judge they would welcome having him home and so the judge found himself begrudgingly granting Dave bail. I was pleased with my success in this traumatizing situation, but I hoped I would not have to experience anything like it ever again.

Members of my chambers did most of the criminal cases in the county of Kent. Nearly all of us did both prosecution and defence, and it was fairly routine for trials to have the prosecution represented by one member of chambers while the defence was represented by another member of the same chambers. This was possible because we were all self-employed and were not part of a firm or partnership or corporation. We merely shared a clerk as a kind of booking agent and office manager for each of us individually. In the circumstances there was deemed to be no conflict of interest. On the whole I enjoyed doing jury trials, and believe I performed better for the defence rather than the prosecution. As defence counsel it was my job to do my best for my clients, without ever misleading the court regarding anything I knew as fact.

But working with the police whenever I was acting as a prosecutor was a real eye-opener for me. My father, as a left-wing politician and someone who had relished his involvement in the early anti-nuclear demonstrations, had always taught me to be wary of anything said in front of the police as he said they often twisted things out of recognition. With that background it was a pleasure for me to develop my own huge respect for the work the police did, and to appreciate society's reliance on them in our frequent need for their services.

In most of the criminal cases I did both for prosecution and defence, the police were excellent. Sadly, there were situations, especially in London, where the police had developed a reputation at that time for moulding the truth to suit their narrative, so much so that juries were reluctant to believe them, and convictions were more difficult to achieve. Through those experiences I became very aware of how valuable it is to live in a society where the police do their jobs as we expect of them and are trusted.

The barrister friend with whom I shared an office in chambers had been asked to write a textbook on criminal proceedings and I declined her invitation to co-author it with her. She not only did an excellent job of that book, but subsequently went on to become the most highly regarded female judge of criminal cases in Britain, eventually narrowly missing becoming Lord Chief Justice, a position to which no female has yet been appointed. My rejection of her invitation to collaborate on the law book is something I have regretted in the years since then as showing less than one hundred percent dedication to my career as well as a missed opportunity to expand my horizons.

My best work was definitely in the field of family law. I had turned down the chance of studying it as an elective because I wanted a general practice and did not want to be type-cast as a typical female, the general attitude being that family law suited the "female temperament". But in reality that was where my passion lay. Solicitors who trusted my judgement would bring their clients to meet me early on in the proceedings so that I could really understand what the most valued outcome for the client was. Once that was understood I would devise a long-term strategy which would be followed to the letter by the solicitor and client in gathering the evidence, and then by me in the courtroom proceedings. On several occasions I had the opportunity to help develop new precedents in the British Court of Appeal, which had direct implications for subsequent cases of a similar nature.

~

Chapter 13 – Marriage

I was certainly happy in my work during those years. I was equally lucky in my living accommodation. My father had left me with money in a trust fund, so that I would have the income it produced but any capital expenditure by me had to be approved by the trustees appointed by him, until my thirtieth birthday. With their support I was able to buy a pretty little terraced Victorian house in the trendy neighbourhood of Notting Hill Gate. I was exceptionally fortunate. Although I had not wanted to live by myself it was a pleasure to be able to give hospitality to many friends and I was often able to find tenants or friends to fill the two spare bedrooms.

The house enabled me to enjoy a wonderful social life. The first party in that house took place on the first day I moved in – 7 July 1971. Everything was so new that, much to my guests' surprise, the bathroom door could not close fully as it was_blocked by a roll of carpet lying in its path! The many parties that followed were so successful that many of my friends came to know each other through those occasions.

Another aspect of my social life involved ski vacations in the Alps. I loved taking the train from London, making new friends during the journey, dancing all night long in the disco car of the train, arriving in a resort in Switzerland, France or Austria the following morning and, after checking in to my accommodation, skiing all day long. I would often go up ski lifts by myself and after forming a new friendship on the lift, would spend the rest of any particular day skiing with that person. And these new-found friends might come from anywhere in the world, including one former Olympian from South America with whom I enjoyed a day of exceptionally courageous skiing!

One such holiday was so successful that a couple of new friends got engaged and invited me to their wedding one year later.

It was at their wedding that I met my future husband Ross when he, a dashing and handsome stranger, had strode across the crowded room to ask me for a dance. Soon after that we became a couple and enjoyed a very social life together both in London and also on many shared ski trips.

During the third year of our relationship our mothers, who had been eager to meet each other for the first time, both died within one month of each other, each from cancer. Within a year after the passing of our mothers, leaving both of us as adult orphans, we decided it was time for us to get married.

I had been so close to my mother that she chose to leave Lattenbells to me in her will. It was a big new responsibility, a five-bedroomed house set in several acres of a glorious garden, located eighty

Expulsion

kilometres from London. Ross and I spent most weekends there while we lived and had our careers in the capital.

My mother and I had been so mutually dependant that I had felt like the traditional spinster daughter whose parent is so reliant on them that they can never have a fully independent life. My name for myself was "Dutiful Daughter", and sometimes I felt envy towards my brother and sister who were free to live into their own young adult lives. I had been unsure that I would ever be able to marry while my mother was alive.

She had lived with leukemia for the previous few years. We had been aware that our time together was limited, and for the last month of her life I nursed her at home in Lattenbells having taken temporary leave from my legal practice. When the end finally came it was devastating for me. During the year after her passing, I thought of her every single day, and had long silent conversations with her.

Aged thirty-two and grieving the loss of my mother, I returned to my childhood condition of sleepwalking. This provided many amusing stories. The most notorious happened during the night after a friend's wedding; I left our hotel bedroom without clothes and roamed along the corridor even venturing down the stairs towards the front desk before Ross could drag me back to the room.

My wedding day was somewhat unusual in a variety of ways. We walked together from my house in Notting Hill Gate to our small registry office wedding with just twelve of us present. Our photographer, well-known for his portraits but inexperienced with weddings, was unable to find the address until after we had left. This was followed by a wonderful lunch hosted by my brother at a small hotel next to Harrods. After an afternoon siesta, Ross played a squash match, saying it was important to start as you meant to continue. That evening we hosted a very informal party for all our friends. His squash opponent arrived in the middle of the party slightly incredulous that it really was our wedding day.

A year later Ross left his job as a consulting civil engineer to pursue a one-year intensive MBA course at Cranfield, Bedfordshire. Happily, during that year I became pregnant for the first time. I was overjoyed.

One Friday evening on the drive from London to Lattenbells we had a conversation that changed my life.

Ross: *"Now you're pregnant we need to think about our children's future. I've just met a business professor from Canada who's visiting at Cranfield. Based on what he says, the future looks brighter in Canada than here in England. I think our children deserve to be Canadian. Let's go look at Canada as soon as I finish my MBA this fall."*

I burst into tears. I was filled with dread. I had been uprooted so many times in my life, and now it was happening again. My marriage had seemed like growing into confirmation of the enviable life we had. I was excited to be starting a family, we had a lovely home in London, Ross could expect good career prospects with his MBA qualification and my law practice was developing well. I thought we were all set for a future with children and our two successful London-based careers, with weekends down in the Sussex countryside and our extended families nearby.

However I had been painfully aware that Ross was not enthusiastic about any of the beautiful family houses we were considering buying in Kensington and he had seemed to my surprise not to have confidence in that future. I had been sufficiently unsure of our future that I had secretly qualified as a solicitor so I would be able to work locally in case our family life would be at Lattenbells and the travel involved in my legal practice as a London-based barrister would become too exhausting. Nevertheless, I had not imagined that we would be choosing a whole new and unfamiliar world. I had visited Canada for one winter week aged thirteen when my brother was an undergraduate in Montreal. Much as I had enjoyed that week, there had been nothing in the experience that made me want to become Canadian. Ross had never visited the country, so his enthusiasm seemed even more difficult to comprehend.

His reaction to my sobbing was not the least bit comforting.

Ross: "*I've been warned that pregnancy makes women even more emotional.*"

Since my pregnancy would prevent me enjoying skiing in the Alps that Christmas, I suggested visiting my relatives from South Africa now living in Toronto. Above all I wanted us to find a home somewhere both of us could envisage a good family life. I intended to practise law wherever we lived, and since I was hoping for a second child before my return to work, it seemed to make sense to take two years away from my London practice to give this Canadian experience a chance. My chambers were quite happy to keep my position open until it was clear if I wanted to return.

As soon as we arrived in Canada Ross worked tirelessly to secure a job that would give us permanent residency. When Ross asked in Toronto how he could get employment, he was told that since the Calgary economy was booming and since he was an engineer, he would get a job even if the only positive thing about him was that he was alive! We flew to Calgary for skiing at nearby Lake Louise, and then during our short twenty-four hours in the city, Montreal Engineering gave him that vital offer of employment.

Aside from Ross' employment opportunity in Calgary, we also chose the province of Alberta because I would be able to practise law in the years before becoming a Canadian citizen, unlike in Ontario and British Columbia. At the end of a wonderful holiday we flew home and submitted our Canadian residency application.

During those final months in London I gave birth to our first child, Clara in April while busily packing up all our worldly possessions. Clara's birth and my becoming a mother was just as life-altering and amazing as I had always imagined it would be, and so much more. I felt instinctively and with enormous gratitude that my mother's love for me translated directly into my love for my children.

Expulsion

We had been advised that even if we were not sure how long we would stay, yet it was more likely for the move to be successful if we travelled like a tortoise, ensuring we had a somewhat permanent home and were surrounded by all our dearest possessions. With that in mind we took with us everything but the proverbial kitchen sink including antique furniture inherited from both our families as well as the King family library consisting of several hundred books.

So it was that in September 1981 at the age of thirty-four, with baby Clara just five months old, I became a Canadian immigrant.

~

Chapter 14 – Arrival in Canada

In the fall of 1981, two weeks after arriving in Canada we bought a recreational property in the mountain town of Canmore. A few weeks later we also bought a family house in Calgary. Our purchases were made despite the fact that it was very uncertain whether we would stay in Canada or would eventually return "home" to England.

Our Calgary house purchase turned into a fiasco in the short term. Calgary's economy was booming, with engineers being brought in from all over the world. Our realtor took advantage of being the only person we knew by keeping me uninformed and dependant on her alone. For example she told me that I could not go to open houses as they were for realtors only, and that there was no such thing as a surveyor's report. On the day the purchase was completed I was astonished when the seller's paralegal personally handed me a surveyor's report with the keys showing that the garden was one quarter the size legally that it appeared on the ground, with the remaining three quarters being designated a roadway! Despite frantic efforts to find alternative resolutions to the problem, nothing was possible except moving into the house, and making the best of the situation. My many previous experiences of being an outsider proved to be helpful in enabling me to understand why our best interests were not top of mind to our new-found connections in this booming city.

Eventually we came to love our house and were delighted with our choice, staying there for over twenty years. We were able to purchase the roadway allowance from the City for a reasonable price after a five-year negotiation, and every member of the family took full advantage of that beautiful garden. We also loved the neighbourhood, which we had chosen with excellent advice given as part of the sales pitch some nine months earlier persuading Ross to move the family to Calgary. When the realtor had told me that this inner-city neighbourhood of Rideau-Roxboro was a great place to bring up a family with an excellent public elementary school, I never imagined staying there long enough for that to be relevant.

Throughout that first long hard winter I was on my own at home with baby Clara and no social connections whatsoever while Ross worked incredibly long hours downtown. Having to pass the Alberta driver's test was made somewhat easier since constant aimless driving reduced Clara's crying. And I learned to navigate the city at the same time. I had thought I would get a nanny as soon as we were settled so I could start work on becoming an Alberta lawyer, but it turned out that there were no Canadian nannies at that time in Calgary and in order to get one it was necessary to import one, preferably from England or the Philippines. So my return to work was delayed until my nanny arrived the following spring. My other major task that winter was buying furniture for the condo townhouse in Canmore, virtually all of which we transported in our new Honda Civic on our one hundred kilometres Friday evening drives to Canmore.

Our neighbours were kind and friendly, but I was in the middle of learning so much, being new in Canada, being a first-time Mom, having no grandparents anywhere, having no nearby family members, being a family person rather than a career woman, and coping with many months of a brutal Canadian winter. I was constantly bombarding them with question after question, and real friendships were still some way in the future.

On the one hand I wanted to return to my London career, to my extended family, to the seasons and the scenery I loved so much, to familiarity. On the other hand I accepted new opportunities in Calgary that started digging me into the community.

At the first meeting of the condo corporation in Canmore I was chosen as secretary, a role I could easily fulfill. In Rideau-Roxboro I enquired to whom I should pay money to join the community association. I was the first person ever to do so, and they were so surprised and delighted that they persuaded me to join the board the following summer. My offers to volunteer in London had never been received with such open enthusiasm, and I was thrilled to find such acceptance.

In order for me to be Called to the Bar in Alberta I had to complete six months of articles as well as passing university examinations in Constitutional Law, Conflict of Laws and Land Titles.

Expulsion

It was tough finding a law firm to offer me articles, both because law firms did not want a woman lawyer and also because I was then pregnant with my second child. Eventually I was able to join the only women-only law firm, Helmer and Martinson, where I fitted in really well.

It so happened that my baby's due date was in late January, before the end of my six months of articles. The Law Society rules dictated that I had to request permission to take time away from doing articles, so, somewhat tongue-in-cheek, I wrote asking for permission for time off in order to give birth. The Law Society's response was that permission could only be granted with specified dates. I responded that as soon as Mother Nature had caught up with the Law Society I would let them know!

As it happened my son Jeremy was born unexpectedly during the evening of Christmas Eve, a month earlier than anticipated. His arrival happened when we had just returned home from one seasonal neighbourhood party and were about to embark on the second party. In the circumstances he was nearly born in the car on the way to the hospital in the snowy back lane. Luckily there was a hospital just minutes away, with a trainee doctor available for instant baby delivery. The next time I saw my baby after his birth was when they woke me at midnight and showed me the Santa sack at the foot of the bed which contained his tiny perfect form!

In early January I attended the required Bar Admissions course, luckily in a hotel a few blocks from my home, so that I did not miss even one day of my articles for maternity leave.

Helmer and Martinson offered to have me stay on with them when I was fully qualified, but exceptionally high interest rates on the firm's debts made this an uneconomical proposition, and I was obliged to look elsewhere. With limited local connections, I ended up with my own sole practice sharing space with two lawyers and an accountant.

Unfortunately, practising law with my own small firm held few of the attractions of my London experience. In London I had been in court almost every day enjoying the cut and thrust of advocacy, legal manoeuvres and cross-examination as well as the fellowship of the Bar. By contrast in Calgary I had little relevant experience to share with clients, I spent most of my time on administrative details while my court appearances were rare, the practice was extremely competitive and the only lawyers with real standing were those who, unlike me, were capable of nurturing big oil companies.

In London legal questions about crime, family law and landlord and tenant were considered to be fascinating questions for society to ponder and debate. In Calgary, especially during a big downturn in the local economy impacting everyone, the focus was much more on maximizing one's earning potential. I gave up my private legal practice after a couple years.

Expulsion

I felt that I had sacrificed my career as an English barrister because of wanting to have a family, so it made little sense to continue developing a new law practice when the time devoted to that was preventing me from full enjoyment of parenting my two adorable children. The Law Society was happy for me to continue my credentials as a practising lawyer through my being a corporate lawyer for the small family company that I had recently set up.

On one of my sister's visits she remarked that we seemed to have reversed the expectations of each of us, with her having a successful career and me having a wonderful family life. I was delighted at her assessment of my family life, while on the other hand, somewhat horrified that she saw my career as being a thing of the past.

~

Chapter 15 – My Immigrant Experience

My sister told me that she was missing my involvement in the property development business in Brighton that she and I and our brother had inherited. I had enjoyed being a company director and had even worked in the office for a short while, but, believe it or not, being actively involved in business had been discouraged by the English Bar as it was considered "conduct unbecoming a barrister"!

After some closer examination it turned out that our manager had developed a secret parallel business which was in competition with us for new property development projects. He was using our credit rating to enable his new acquisitions. Unravelling the resulting mess with the assistance of lawyers and accountants necessitated numerous trips to England over the next few years.

I decided to take the opportunity to unravel the complex extended family corporate structure set up by my father and transform my minority share into cash. I did not want my children's future to be determined by what happened in faraway Brighton and for them to have their financial priorities set by whichever of their English cousins would eventually be responsible for managing the business.

Expulsion

At the start our professional advisors had advised that it would not be possible to properly value individual shareholdings within the multi-layered ownership structures and to untangle the ownership without sacrificing everything to taxation. However eventually I was able to draft a foundational agreement enabling each of the three of us to achieve our individual priorities. The leading lawyer was sufficiently impressed to enquire if I would like to join their firm, which I declined while finding the comment very flattering. At the end of those three years I felt a huge sense of pride that I had been able to "bring home the bacon" for my own nuclear family.

The cash I received enabled me to set up a family company in Calgary. It seemed fitting for Ross to become president of our new company since he had lost his job in the economic downturn. With his civil engineering and my legal backgrounds it made sense for us to start doing a series of small inner-city property developments together. This also enabled us both to work from home and to enjoy our children, with me in the main parenting role. The downside was that it effectively ended our professional careers, which we had both treasured.

My memory of those years of family life was one filled with a lot of happiness and a feeling that this really was what life was supposed to be all about. And yet I had a personal obsession to find a new career path. I had to balance needing the challenge and prestige of a rewarding career, with the fact that the children needed me, and financially I could manage without a career because of the money I had inherited coupled with the income produced by our small family business.

Much as I loved this life I was determined not to dominate my children's lives by living my life only through theirs. I did not want to repeat my mother's extreme focus on me, kind-hearted as she had been. This may also have been a rationalization since my energy and drive coupled with the warm response I received from those with whom I volunteered pushed me towards huge amounts of volunteer activities. The community became like a replacement for my faraway extended family.

Baking with Jeremy and Clara

I was delighted at the sense of social responsibility that surrounded me. Whether it was a question of responding to a request to raise our outside mailbox to a level that would reduce the chance of injury to our "postie", or learning not to damage people's lawns by crossing

Expulsion

their unfenced front gardens, or stopping for pedestrians at any unmarked intersection, all these small acts were new expectations. I was constantly learning wonderful life lessons from my neighbours who were more community minded than anyone I had previously met.

One day a previously unknown neighbour came to our door, saying that she understood from researching educational records that we had a child eligible for kindergarten. She explained that if the parents of each such child in the neighbourhood agreed to jointly petition the Board of Education for a new kindergarten class at our school, one would be added. I was so impressed that I cancelled my previous choice of the school in the adjoining community and went along with the neighbourhood plan.

When we got our new kindergarten teacher the parents let her know we would happily do any aspect of her job that she found troublesome. The parents explained to me that the more she enjoyed teaching our children, the happier our children would be and that in turn would lead to happier family lives for all of us!

They were patiently teaching me the benefits of living lives in the knowledge that what goes around comes around. It was so simple and yet so profound.

During my year as president of the Rideau-Roxboro Community Association I persuaded some owners to have their properties down-zoned so the whole community would be single-family residential. I encouraged riverbank owners to help the City turn the opposite riverbank from an informal paved parking lot into a grassy park.

Responding to a government invitation to apply for a grant to assist with hiring students for the summer months, I developed a novel drop-

in daycare so new families would have a chance to intermingle with others before school started in the fall.

For three years I led a committee tasked with challenging property tax assessments on behalf of all residents, resulting in significant savings for everyone.

Madeleine on a family Club Med ski trip.

We successfully challenged the proposed closure of our local hospital, the Holy Cross, delaying its eventual closure by at least ten years. As president of the parents' association at Rideau Park School I led the negotiation for a unique multi-year agreement with the Calgary Board of Education ensuring its continuation as a school with classes from kindergarten through to grade nine. We were at the same time able to create amongst the parents such a supportive atmosphere that helped the school be a city-wide magnet for teachers.

Shortly after, I was asked to join the Board of Parents Anonymous – a small non-profit which had developed a respite program for families in times of stress, with the aim of reducing child abuse by offering a safe haven for young children for up to three days at a time. My legal experience in England with child abuse cases which I had found very distressing persuaded me to agree to be involved. Once again I became the society secretary, a role that was easy for me to fulfill. Having soon after read about the opportunities volunteers should have to expand their own horizons by learning new skills, I chose to learn more about fund-raising. During the first year writing a dozen letters which happily brought in sufficient funds was all that was entailed.

A brilliant proposal to establish the respite nursery was developed by a director who was a professor of nursing at the University of Calgary. When we acquired a building and were able to start our respite nursery, known as The Children's Cottage, it became clear that our much-increased fund-raising needs would be more easily met if the Children's Cottage became a separate charitable organization, of which I proudly became the first board chair. One day we were asked by a donor to let him know our five-year goal ignoring financial constraints and the steps we would take to achieve those goals. It was the first time I had ever been able to develop such a visionary plan, and with his assistance we were able to achieve those goals. I was inspired by the opportunity not only to dream of a future but to work collaboratively to achieve it.

There were of course some inevitable initial hiccoughs like agreeing to increase salaries for childcare staff without government agreement or our own available funds, which led to all directors and other volunteers needing to work monthly bingos to bring in instant funds. However we were truly fortunate after the first few months to hire a superb executive director who has remained with the organization, now some thirty years later. We were also fortunate in being able to put together a strong board of directors, supported by enthusiastic funders both government and private.

I loved this work, but it soon became clear how important it is to recognize that being a volunteer board chair is not a career. The role is that of steward of the organization, but its direction and reputation rests in the hands of the professional leader chosen by the board. I still needed to find my own career direction.

One of my other volunteer involvements came about in a somewhat unusual way. In the early hours one night two years before Calgary hosted the 1988 Winter Olympics I wrote out a detailed proposal for how it could be developed as one huge community party and sent it to then Mayor Ralph Klein. Within a few days he arranged for me to explain it to him in his office at the old City Hall. He persuaded me to join a few other volunteers and work with the City administration in developing the first Winter Festival that would act as a dry run for the Olympics. It was my first experience of volunteering with the City's

Expulsion

Parks and Recreation Department and was thoroughly enjoyable. It was mentioned that this might well lead to a permanent role as volunteer chair of a major annual festival. I was intrigued but believed that if I continued to search I would find a broader scope in my future.

When Calgary hosted the Olympics I was keen to enjoy that once-in-a-lifetime experience with my children, then aged seven and six, and so did not participate as a volunteer. Sharing their joy at the events, at meeting mascots Heidi and Howdy, watching PetroCanada's flame-lighting relay, climbing through the ice palace, watching night-time fireworks and so many other fabulous moments of children's delight was a real gift for me.

This was also a turning point for Calgary. The city had placed itself on the world stage, attracting comparisons with other Olympic host cities. Its community and volunteer spirit were shown to be the envy of the world. After the unqualified success of those Olympics I was proud to call myself a Calgarian. The city suffers in some respects because of its being so remote geographically from other major population centres, but it has the benefits accorded to the old city-states, with significant local autonomy, prosperity, and civic pride.

~

Chapter 16 – Finding a Spiritual Home

One surprise of living in Canada was that I found myself profoundly missing living in a country with a national church. Although I had only been an irregular churchgoer during my adult years in England, yet I had found it comforting that it was always available and was part of the shared social experience. For example, I had enjoyed and often been inspired by listening to the Christian stories broadcast for ten minutes every morning on BBC. I had loved joining in singing well-known hymns on random social occasions. Weddings and Christmases were very often occasions to re-immerse myself in the Anglican experience.

So in Calgary I asked a neighbour to take me to a service at our local Anglican church, Christ Church Elbow Park. I enjoyed the service which was led by the charismatic, brilliant, and wise rector, Herb O'Driscoll, a writer of many faith books and hymns as well as a teacher of theologians.

By that time I knew that my spiritual home was in the Anglican Church, but in England I had not been entitled to take communion, a ritual available only to those who were both baptized and confirmed.

Expulsion

By the end of that service I knew that my being accepted as a full member was long overdue. On exiting I introduced myself to Rector Herb, immediately mentioning to him that I wanted to be baptized. He seemed surprised at my determination without my having been a church member.

Hearing my short explanation when we next met, he commented that my faith seemed like an illicit affair, a relationship that I had kept hidden from the world for many years. I then had to admit that I could not attend regular Sunday services or baptism classes since every weekend was spent in Canmore for skiing or hiking! In response to his suggestion that maybe skiing was more important to me than my faith, I quickly told him that it was family life rather than skiing that I needed to prioritize.

Reassured, he suggested I join a small group who attended at six forty-five every Friday morning, a service known as TGIF (Thank God It's Friday). A few years later I was baptized during a beautiful Easter service. I remained an active member of TGIF until it was disbanded some ten years later. After that several of us moved together to a neighbouring parish, and now thirty years later we continue our mutual journey through a wonderful book club.

During the coffee and muffins after each short TGIF service we shared books, newspaper articles and our travel stories, gradually getting to know each other's lives in meaningful ways. That group soon became my "companions on the journey" of a deep and meaningful spiritual life. In later years when I was on my own I welcomed the chance of going on retreats and bus-tour pilgrimages with members of TGIF.

When I had sought out a spiritual home as a young person growing up, no-one had ever explained to me the enormous value of these transformative friendships, based on shared journeys of searching for deeper meaning in the many experiences of our "snakes-and-ladders" journey through life.

~

Chapter 17 – Being a Politician

Having wanted to be a politician for many years, my political career was finally launched in 1993 with a big splash as the Liberal candidate against Alberta Premier Ralph Klein in Calgary Elbow. My father had fought elections all through his life and it had kindled in me a real desire to follow in his footsteps. I had imagined that immigrating to a new country would have killed any such opportunity, but I had misjudged the openness of the Canadian public.

A neighbour had merely persuaded me to intervene in the nomination process for the Liberal candidate, not believing that I would advance further than that stage. However, as soon as I started campaigning I became energized and ambitious.

Surprisingly, in the week before the election Premier Klein's team were so concerned he might lose to me that he publicly proclaimed that if he lost he would quit as Premier of Alberta and leave politics altogether. The day before the election media outlets in the Maritimes were reporting that an upset was a very real possibility, and the CBC as national broadcaster requested an interview the following day in the event of my success. Although Klein had been popular as mayor, he had none of the focus on healthcare, education, culture and statesmanship of long-serving Premier Peter Lougheed. This meant that my team was able to attract great campaign leadership as well as a couple hundred eager volunteers.

Nevertheless for a woman with two young children who had arrived in the country twelve years previously, the response to my campaign seemed quite remarkable!

Although I did not win that election it changed my experience in Calgary in both good and bad ways. The good aspects were that I discovered a real love for campaigning and a great pleasure in engaging with people at their doors; I developed numerous new friendships; my energy and commitment won the respect of many Klein supporters which opened many doors in future years. On the negative side, Klein's chief of staff never forgave me for the anxiety my campaign had caused them, and he took delight in preventing me from receiving any appointment controlled by the provincial government during his long tenure.

One rainy night when I was going door to door with a new volunteer, she made me promise that if I lost that election I would join her as a UNICEF volunteer. I had long been interested in international development and had already been disappointed to discover no volunteer opportunities were available in Calgary with the International Red Cross. Hers was a wonderful invitation that led to my eventually joining te national board of UNICEF, heading up the Alberta region and travelling, on my dime, to view the work UNICEF was doing in Thailand. My fellow volunteers were special Canadians with a commitment to children's welfare and international development.

Leading the Alberta chapter allowed me to forge a close relationship with the executive director and together we transformed it into one of the strongest in Canada. It also proved a great foundation for my later Rotary work shipping hospital equipment to Uganda as well as helping educate hundreds of AIDS orphans and organizing a group of Rotarians to visit.

One evening I was drinking beer in my favourite Calgary pub, *The Dog and Duck*, when some men asked if I would be interested in joining the board of the Airport Authority. They explained that the Federal Government was about to make their first two appointments and they had heard that one was likely to be a woman. I was so enthusiastic that I set about convincing the government that despite a lack of experience of the aviation industry, I was nevertheless the one they should pick for the position. I was successful and enjoyed my board experience enormously.

After a short while the board chair asked me to take over leadership of the governance committee, one of the four standing committees, and I was delighted to accept. However, at the next board meeting he gave the position to someone else, a man. I was horrified that he could treat me so badly. Following the meeting I called the only other woman on the board, asking for her advice as a fellow female. She started by saying she had no advice as a woman, but by the end of a long conversation she said: "*If you were a man Madeleine you would beat him up verbally straight away. You would tell him what you think of his dreadful behaviour to you. You wouldn't let him get away with it.*"

I was grateful for her insight and yet taken aback by the suggestion. I immediately called the board chair berating him and forcing him to apologize. Much to my amazement, not only did he apologize, but he also said he would reinstate the offer to me. Sure enough at the next board meeting he told everyone that he had made a mistake, behaved badly, and would need to find another position for the other man, since that particular job was mine. After that he and I became good friends and worked closely together for the following few years.

My female colleague's advice caused me to abandon my natural tendencies in order to act in a more masculine way, one that felt foreign to me. Yet it clearly worked! The experience definitely alerted me to constant openness to learning how to adapt my behaviour in a man's environment.

During these years, enjoying my new-found connectivity in Calgary, I was also working as a consultant raising funds professionally for various charities.

My personal dream was still to be a politician. The municipal level was attractive both because it was not organized along party political lines and also because most of my volunteering concerned municipal issues.

Expulsion

In 2001 I won the election becoming a city councillor, then known as "Alderman". I almost immediately tried unsuccessfully to change the title to the gender-neutral title of "Councillor"; I was just a few years too early!

Alderman Madeleine with Mayor Dave Bronconnier

I represented about eighty thousand residents in the south-west portion of Calgary's inner-city where I lived. It was incredibly exciting that my personal vision and commitment, with no party affiliation, was able to inspire so many supporters. A truly humbling experience!

At the municipal level it was the first of my three campaigns. In each one I was supported personally by a team of wonderful friends and other volunteers at the same time as being fully funded by donations. It made me very proud!

At City Hall my interest lay in making the city more urban, sustainable, cultural, and diverse.

At that time, the city's growth plans were wholly dependant on greenfield development in the fast-growing new suburbs while inner-city residents of the older communities were paying a disproportionate percentage of the budget. Environmental issues were not yet on the City's front burner. The transportation department was focused on increasing vehicle volume and speed, rather than increasing walkability or cycling. The City's chief planning document was the "Go Plan", focused on going from place to place rather than creating good spaces in which to be. Also, the funding of culture lacked any strategic thinking at City Hall. There was a lot for me to do. It felt like turning the wheel of a big ship to start pointing the city towards a more progressive future.

I was inspired by the urban writer and academic Richard Florida, a regional economist from Pittsburgh whose research showed that it was economically and socially worthwhile to develop a city so that it would be attractive to young leaders of the new economy, his so-called "Creative Class".

Expulsion

As a co-leader of our one-hundred-year sustainability vision for the city, known as ImagineCALGARY, I met, read, and listened to some of the field's most exciting thought-leaders. Responding to concerns of administrative leaders that the final report would be put on a shelf like so many others, I came up with a plan to embed the goals into the city's annual budget and workplans, leading to a special executive team within the city manager's office, which is still operational some fifteen years later. Participating in this initiative was one of the many privileges of being a city councillor.

Working with progressive community leaders I enjoyed the opportunity to play a leadership role in transforming the densely populated area of the Beltline. We reimagined urban parks catering to inner-city residents much less homogeneous than suburban dwellers, and encouraged live music venues, galleries, and other local arts organizations. Developers could increase the number of storeys and include small stores, offices, green roofs, and public art into residential buildings. I was focused on increasing the number of people living, working, and playing in the area, known as "eyes on the street", thereby reducing street crime.

One notable legacy came from my involvement in the arts. Art galleries, classical music, ballet, opera, theatre, and literature had been important pleasures to me since childhood, without my having any artistic ability. City Council gave me leadership of a committee to review civic policies concerning the arts. We invited and got representation from the provincial and federal governments, the major funders, as well as creative and visionary leaders from Calgary's arts companies and civic administration. The group was exceptional, and they reached out to their many connections in the city, across the country and even internationally so that we would have the best input we could possibly wish for. After a few years of hard work the committee's recommendations to City Council were all approved. A new era began for the city's growing cultural community with increased funding and the establishment of a new strategic planning and funding body, the Calgary Arts Development Authority. Soon after I was able to help bring the Junos to Calgary and encouraged the city to become the annually designated Cultural Capital of Canada.

A few years later I joined a group determined to establish Calgary's first public contemporary art gallery. After numerous twists and turns, I was able to play a behind-the-scenes role in ensuring the City made available the former planetarium, a stunning brutalist concrete structure somewhat resembling New York's Guggenheim Museum, and the Contemporary Calgary Gallery was finally launched in the fall of 2019.

The local arts leaders I worked with were creative, visionary, open and great company. Their friendship was one of the best aspects of my years as a civic politician.

Despite Calgary only having one hundred fifty years history in contrast to my Sussex village with a thousand-year history, I discovered how genuine people were in their desire to retain the bricks and mortar that told the story of their and their ancestors' time in this place. I made a particularly significant speech in a Council meeting, telling how great cities are admired because of what landmarks make them unique, and that Calgary should support its own particular history and character. It proved to be the beginning of a grassroots heritage movement which has continued to grow in influence ever since.

I faced many challenges to get inner city projects included in the funding pipeline in a very suburban-oriented city. My proposal for a new railway underpass linking the redevelopment area of the East Village with the Stampede grounds was initially disqualified from funding since its aim was to link two otherwise disconnected communities, and not to increase the flow and speed of vehicles. Fortunately and despite much opposition, I was soon able to demonstrate how valuable this link would be, and so the funding was eventually found, and the underpass built.

Traffic circles were new to Calgary. Since this new trend had echoes of British roundabouts, and since I still had an English accent my supposed influence on the introduction of traffic circles made me the target of many an irate driver unsure of how to behave going round one of these new-fangled obstacles!

During my six years on City Council I worked long hours averaging about eighty to ninety hours per week. My personal life became completely submerged under my political life. I was in the news almost every day and became very experienced with television, radio, and newspaper interviews, some even in French.

My face and voice were so well known locally that I was recognized and talked to wherever I went, whether in taxis, groceries stores, gas stations, church, parties, even at passport control or on plane journeys to Europe. On the one hand I relished being seen as someone capable of making a difference in people's lives and their community. On the other hand it became impossible to carry on other personal relationships.

My marriage came to an end one year after I was elected to City Council, by which time fortunately both children were away at university. There are always many reasons for such breakdowns, but I believe one was that it was tough socially for him when my opinions were constantly sought as a decision-maker with power to make a difference in people's lives. Like many others who have lived through such personal heartache, I have found it difficult not to replay how my behaviour, if different, might have brought about a better outcome.

My English family expected me to take the opportunity to return to live in England. But I was totally immersed locally and in representing thousands of people, and however lonely my personal life might be, there was little time for it outside of my working hours. Additionally, like so many others who have come to Calgary from elsewhere, I had a passion for the city. I cherished its energy and sense that together we were co-creating a place where everyone was welcomed and encouraged in making a future of their choosing.

Towards the end of my first three-year term I started reassembling my campaign team and was eagerly looking forward to the adrenaline-

Expulsion

rush leading up to an election. On a quiet summer day I went for a regular annual mammogram feeling fit and healthy with a huge long list of things that needed doing. To my utter amazement I was told I was pre-cancerous. I could not believe it was happening to me. It just did not seem possible. This was the start of an emotional roller-coaster.

A lumpectomy was prescribed, and I was told it could wait until after the election in the fall. My two children were both outstanding in their care for me, each one coming to Calgary to help care for me. Both my brother and sister made time out of their busy lives in England to come stay with me and look after me.

One of the big questions was with whom else I should share this information. Ethical answers from across North America indicated that you should disclose to your potential employer at the interview stage any surgery or other time away from work you would require after starting a new job. It seemed clear to me that the public were my potential employer and so I decided it was only right to share the news with everyone.

People were amazingly kind and considerate. One aspect I had not foreseen was that many of them shared their own cancer journeys with me, some being very confidential and intimate. I felt pleased to be able to bring the comfort of sharing to many, and humbled to become a public face for the breast cancer journey. For example, I was the first recipient of an official pink Stampede hat kicking off a season of recognition and donations.

124

In the following months I had two lumpectomies and then major surgery. It was certainly a very tough year, but I was fortunate to have treatments with good eventual outcomes without the need for any radiation, chemotherapy, or subsequent years of drug therapy. Although my cancer journey was a relatively short one, yet I felt the experience changed me. I became more deeply grounded in gratitude for each passing day, and for loved ones and my many friendships and opportunities.

The fact that my personal journey with cancer was essentially all over within one year and did not leave me struggling to regain lost energy, made me feel unworthy to continue as a public champion. My experience was so much less harsh than that for so many others.

I was busy as a city councillor throughout my procedures and recovery except for short periods of recuperation. After that year, my term continued until the next election in the fall of 2007. My campaign team was excellent, and I received more donations than any other member of council.

It was a very hard-fought campaign and a narrow result, but the outcome was that I surrendered my seat on City Council. My defeat in that election came as a shock to me, and to many others too.

It was the end of an era for me. However, I was exceptionally fortunate that all the civic causes I had championed with such passion proved to be the foundations that the next mayor and council continued to build on for the following decade.

Chapter 18 – My '*Under the Tuscan Sun*' Years

In the fall of 2007 I cleared my desk at City Hall, emailed all City staff to let them know what a privilege it had been working with them, thanked my volunteers for a wonderful team effort and contemplated my new life.

I was shattered!

One of the things that made a huge difference to my mood was the outpouring of appreciative letters and cards, all of which I collected in a special binder. Those letters mean so much to me.

Luckily, after the election I was able to accompany a friend to an international conference in Madrid where I could spend long days alone in art galleries considering the meaning of life and other such deep questions.

My cancer experience had taught me to appreciate the experience of every day. Now I needed to live fully into every moment of aliveness. And to treasure every loving relationship. As a young person I had fantasized about making a difference in the global sense. When I went into politics my goal was to make a difference for thousands of

Calgary citizens. Now I was able to realize that if I could still make a difference in the life of any one person that would be a goal worth striving for. I also realized my great good fortune, that I now had good health, loving children and close family, a lovely home, wonderful friends, the ability to travel, and enough money to put plentiful food on the table. I read with interest the book "The Power of Now" by Eckhart Tolle and I strove to live into its wisdom.

I now needed to earn a living, especially because of bad advice and bad decisions during the financial crash of 2007. Having embarked on a master's degree in environmental design shortly before leaving City Hall, I planned to work in the field of urban planning based on my business and municipal government experience. Fortunately on my return from Madrid a developer asked me to be the consultant for properties on Mission Road in Calgary's inner-city, where he and others had independently bought nearly all the houses years earlier believing that its strategic location would lead to development potential. With his help I formed an urban planning consultancy with the specific aim of assisting clients as they manoeuvred through the processes of City Hall. Since I had just moved into a beautiful new home I was able to work from a home-office.

My consultancy occupied my working life for about ten years. Clients ranged from property developers negotiating with City administration, to developers arguing with residents neighbouring prospective projects, to community activists resisting change in their neighbourhoods. While some clients were wholly dependant on my

Expulsion

work for them, others taught me a great deal by bringing a range of business skills and experience to the table.

When I left City Hall I had just built a house specially designed for me by architect and friend Jeremy Sturgess. What an incredible privilege to be able to live in a stunning environment, with views of the Beltline and Downtown, in vibrant colours I had wanted since I was three years old and with welcoming entertaining space that transformed my single life! For example I had previously discovered that I was always disorganized for my dinner parties so it was important that guests could enjoy their appetizers in the same space where I was cooking. Similarly since I preferred to linger around a large dining table, it had to occupy a central area of the main room. I had always loved open wood-burning fires, so my fireplace had to be sufficiently easy to start and to store firewood that I could manage it on my own. It was life-changing since guests so enjoyed spending time in the space that invitations to a broad range of acquaintances as well as those to close friends were always eagerly accepted. What a gift!

One experience of my living in the house involved a neighbour erecting an ugly little white painted wooden windmill on top of a tall tree stump directly in my view. My request to him for it to be lowered so it might impact his view more than mine was met with uncompromising hostility. In the months and years following, surprisingly I came to love watching the antics of squirrels jumping from nearby trees and utility poles onto the platform. They built their nests in the windmill, and then protected and fed their babies there. Eventually they loved the windmill so much they chewed the wood until first one and then a second and third arm of the windmill fell off, and the whole thing finally fell into the neighbour's garden in pieces.

The lesson I drew from all of this was that I was fortunate enough, especially as a woman, to be able to control what happened in my own home, but I had no such power over what happened outside my own property. So I should celebrate what I did have, and not fret about what I could not influence!

Happily, my daughter Clara in Vancouver saw how good life was in Calgary and she returned to pursue her career goals here, and some years later married and settled down close by. My son Jeremy was able to complete two degrees in Boston where he met and married, had a family, and found a good life.

One of the amazing aspects of my new home was that I had chosen to build it on a lot adjacent to two unique houses owned by friends who became my chosen family. For the previous fifteen years they had shared friends and families with each other, so there was a whole clan associated with them, many of whom had already become my friends. They were generous to a fault, loved the mountains, the arts, interesting young people, politics, international travel and parties. Their friendship and warm inclusion of me in their lives enabled me to have the best life imaginable given my single status. It had echoes of the life portrayed in the movie "Under the Tuscan Sun" based on the book by Frances Mayes.

Expulsion

I continued to travel and volunteer my time extensively. I was very active in my Rotary club as well as becoming board chair of Bethany Care Society, a large faith-based organization focused on continuing care for frail seniors. Since that time I have enjoyed the collegiality of both, have been inspired by their vision and have been kept fully engaged with the challenges each brings with it.

During those years without a partner I tried never to travel by myself, but would go with my neighbours, with Rotary both to do projects and to visit Rotarians around the world, with Clara and also with my brother and his wife. I also visited England, Scotland, and Ireland as much as I could and stayed with family and friends. My American grandchildren were and will always be a huge draw too.

My relationship with my children blossomed during these years. When Clara suffered a bad ski accident she needed to move back home, and I was able to "mother" her for many months. When she had to give herself daily injections into her stomach, I would lead her in singing "Nine green bottles" so she would forget her anxiety, even if only for a fleeting moment, and have the courage to plunge the needle in. Despite the difficulties of those months we laughed a lot together and learned to enjoy living companionably as two adults. When she became Assistant Minister at nearby St. Stephens Anglican Church I followed her there so I could enjoy her beautiful presence and inspiring sermons.

With Jeremy I spent many special weekends in the States, debating through the night his university syllabus, his political views and his career aspirations. With his many friends we had wonderful dinners and even an international vacation. Two of his friends worked for me as summer students at City Hall, while they and Jeremy stayed with me.

When the happy moments came for each of them to get married, I was able to be there for them, and to feel the warmth of our love for each other.

~

Chapter 19 – Romance

On July 1st, Canada Day 2016 there was a huge celebratory opening of Calgary's new National Music Centre and I was a proud participant. What a fabulous building, totally unlike anything seen before in Calgary! I was mingling with fellow Rotarians when the subject of good dance places came into the conversation. It was agreed we would meet up on Sunday afternoon July 10 to dance at a Bowness pub and to celebrate my seventieth birthday. All Rotary friends were immediately invited, and it was suddenly clear I was going to be very public about sharing this milestone, something I had not previously contemplated.

The next celebration was to be *the big one*, which I had been planning for the past two years. Some twenty-five of my family members gathered in the South of France for a few days of merriment. Each small group rented their own accommodation in Collioure on the Mediterranean near the Spanish border, which I knew well and had visited frequently. We were all within easy walking distance of each other and of all the restaurants and beaches we frequented during those magical days. The date had been specially chosen to coincide with an amazing annual fireworks display overlooking the bay with the medieval fort, fishing port and beach.

The meticulous planning on my part had included a special visit to the town a year earlier to make a personal plea for a table for twenty-five at a quayside restaurant on that evening. When my request to various locations had been flatly refused, it made me enraged on the subject of the local mentality. However, I then realized that one of the great charms of that area is that there are no tour buses, no hotel chains, and no national stores. That is in fact a big reason why I love it so much. In that context it made sense that they did not welcome a large group reservation, and I came to respect them for their attitude. The following spring I called the restaurant owner from Canada, and in my broken French asked him if he had sourced his ingredients for the fireworks evening yet and if he was satisfied now with his menu preparation. Finally, he was won over by my passion for the cause and my obvious love of his location.

A Calgary friend, Eileen, and I set off in early August flying to Toulouse where we rented a car. We had a fabulous time in nearby Bordeaux both in the medieval city and tasting wine nearby, we visited the coastal resort of Biarritz and then crossed over into Spain to stay at San Sebastien. Its glorious location in addition to some of the most creative cuisine I have ever experienced made our visit special. We were also able to visit Bilbao with its magnificent Guggenheim museum. In Spain we purchased a carload of child and grandparent-friendly beach equipment and games for our time in Collioure.

Expulsion

When we finally reached Collioure in France we discovered that terrorism had forced the town to cancel the famous fireworks! The threat forced the deployment of a significant number of armed police, whose presence in large numbers everywhere reassured us that we would at least be safe. And eventually the restaurant owner was delighted that we were there enjoying copious amounts of his food and wine, since there were not many other visitors. Few of my guests had previously seen the fireworks and so they did not mind their absence. After the meal we stayed late into the evening dancing on the quayside and expressing our gratitude to the armed guards that were keeping us safe.

One of the many reasons for my happiness at that time was that I was developing a special friendship that felt like the early stages of romance.

Two years earlier on a bus pilgrimage to Ireland with my friend Helen, a group of five from Calgary frequently enjoyed tasting Irish whiskey together before dinner. One of the members of that group was Bob, a widower grieving the recent loss of his wife.

The following spring on another bus pilgrimage (this time to the Holy Land with Elizabeth, my daughter's mother-in-law) who should be amongst the small contingent from Calgary again but Bob. A friendship slowly developed. Although on the couple of occasions that Bob asked me for a drink, others would inevitably join us, never suspecting that we might prefer to spend the evening alone.

On our return we started hiking together in the mountains. I was amazed that he had the patience to accommodate his pace to my slowness, and that for hours on end we could thoroughly enjoy each other's company.

At Clara's encouragement I had decided to host a large party in early September at my home in Calgary, celebrating my birthday and also the fact I had lived exactly half my life in Calgary. So as not to be confused with my 70th birthday celebration this was billed as my *35 Plus 35* party.

Much to my surprise and delight Bob offered to help me prepare the food for the anticipated one hundred guests. Those two days we worked together wove their magic in cementing the budding romance. However the hiccoughs were not yet over.

Just like our friends in the Holy Land, my party guests were totally blind to the possibility of this relationship. They were oblivious to the thought we might want to be together and so towards the end of the party they drew me into an intimate huddle away from Bob, who quietly departed.

Apart from a brief email exchange later that night there was no way to retrieve the lost special time that we each had hoped would continue the growth of our romance. Worse, the following day I was flying to Las Vegas with a friend celebrating her eightieth birthday. This was followed by the fact that just when I returned to Calgary Bob was flying off to Abbotsford, BC, for an aunt's funeral!

Expulsion

Finally, when Bob let me know he was at Calgary Airport I asked him to come over straightaway, and we have been together ever since. A year later we were married at our newly shared spiritual home of St. Stephens in the presence of many of our family and friends.

October 7, 2017

I could never have imagined that my seventieth birthday would be the catalyst for a whole new phase of my life, and that I would be lucky enough to find such joy.

~

Chapter 20 – Final Thoughts
... For Now

A few years ago my son Jeremy told me he had developed a personal mission statement. Considering the possibility to formulate in mid-life what I thought I knew about my values seemed an interesting opportunity. So I worked at developing one that satisfies me, and I keep it by my side, which means it is written in my phone notes. It tells me I must use the talents God gave me to contribute and make a difference in the lives of others, and to treasure those I love – my husband, family, and close friends. And, of course, there is always time for fun, excitement, and joy.

Having now both retired from paid employment, Bob and I enjoy our extensive travels. In the past couple of years, before the COVID19 pandemic temporarily stopped us in our tracks, we have cycled in Germany, walked a part of the Camino de Santiago in Spain, travelled in Switzerland, Italy and France with my step-grandchildren, visited England several times and India twice. As well we have participated in international development projects in two hospitals in India and acquired a donated fire truck for Guatemala.

Our adult children and their children give me great joy, both all those living nearby as well as those in Boston.

In 2019 Bob delighted and surprised me by nominating me for a Calgary Immigrants of Distinction award in the lifetime achievement category. Not only was it wonderful to have him pay so much attention to my past, but it was also very special when I was chosen as a finalist and celebrated the awards gala evening surrounded by family and friends.

2019 Immigrant of Distinction Awards

Expulsion

And now the pandemic of 2020 has caused us all to wonder what life will look like in its new reality. And for myself, who knows what the next chapter may bring?

My path through life has felt like a "Plan B" development, with resilience constantly needed in order to celebrate outcomes often least expected.

Madame Palisch's prediction conveyed to my father all those years ago was that I would end up in the gutter.

I am so glad that my life so far has proven her completely wrong!

~